THE BLACK-OUT BOOK

One-hundred-and-one
black-out nights' entertainment

OSPREY
PUBLISHING

THE BLACK-OUT BOOK

One-hundred-and-one black-out nights' entertainment

Compiled by
Evelyn August

Drawings by
Woods

Introduction by
Mike Brown

Incorporating
"Strictly Personal"
and
"A—Zoo"
by
Muriel and Sydney Box

First published in Great Britain in 2009 by Osprey Publishing, Midland House,
West Way, Botley, Oxford OX2 0PH, United Kingdom.
443 Park Avenue South, New York, NY 10016, USA.
Email: info@ospreypublishing.com

A CIP catalog record for this book is available from the British Library.

ISBN: 978 1 84603 923 2

Originated by PDQ Media, Bungay, UK
Printed in China through Worldprint Ltd

09 10 11 12 13   10 9 8 7 6 5 4 3 2 1

For a catalog of all books published by Osprey please contact:

NORTH AMERICA
Osprey Direct, c/o Random House Distribution Center
400 Hahn Road, Westminster, MD 21157, USA
E-mail: uscustomerservice@ospreypublishing.com

ALL OTHER REGIONS
Osprey Direct, The Book Service Ltd., Distribution Centre,
Colchester Road, Frating Green, Colchester, Essex, CO7 7DW
E-mail: customerservice@ospreypublishing.com

www.ospreypublishing.com

INTRODUCTION

W HEN the Wright Brothers, Wilbur and Orville, made the first powered flight on 17 December 1903, the world could little guess that they would change the face of warfare so drastically. However, when, just over ten years later, World War I, or the Great War as it was then known, broke out, aircraft were soon seen as wonderful vehicles for observing the enemy's movements.

Lighting restrictions, as a measure primarily against observation from the air, were first introduced to Britain in areas around harbours, as early as August 1914, and were extended to the whole country one month later. These lighting restrictions were soon nicknamed the 'black-out', and the name took hold of the public imagination. What at first was seen as a nuisance became grim necessity when, on 19 January 1915, in a deadly shift of tactics, a bombing raid by German Zeppelins, huge dirigible balloons, on the town of King's Lynn in Norfolk killed two people and injured thirty; death from the air had come to Britain, and from this point no civilian in wartime could feel truly safe in his or her bed.

Twenty years later, war once again threatened to engulf Britain, and the government planners resurrected the idea of the black-out. As early as 1936 the Home Office prepared an order, to be implemented in time of war, under which all street lighting and motor vehicle headlamps were banned and which required the screening of all interior lights.

These black-out regulations came into force on 1 September 1939, as war with Germany rapidly approached. The details of the regulations involved were based on the experience of flyers in World War I, when aircraft flew at less than a hundred miles an hour and so low that pilots could see a match being struck in the trenches below; indeed in 1939 it did become illegal to light a cigarette in the now pitch-dark streets, where once-familiar journeys became mystery tours. Street lights were out of the question, and vehicles of all descriptions had to negotiate the streets with headlights heavily shrouded, while white lines were painted down the centre of roads and round trees and lamp-posts in an attempt to avoid accidents.

For pedestrians, none but the weakest torches could be used to help find their way, and only then if covered with several layers of tissue paper and never, never pointed upwards, unless one wanted to risk being arrested and held under suspicion of being a Fifth Columnist attempting to signal to the German Air Force. Deaths on the road increased massively and any journey at night became a hazardous trek, to be avoided whenever possible.

Thus, during the winter of 1939/40, it became common practice to stay in at night. In the event dreaded air-raids failed to materialize, at least their non-appearance meant that staying at home could, on the whole, be done in the comfort of one's living room; the delights of shelter life would wait until 1940.

In these first few months of war, ways of whiling away the hours of black-out were sought. Advertisements held up chemistry sets and model kits as interesting and educational ways to make the most of the black-out hours, while a rash of books especially written for the purpose were published, with titles such as *Arthur Mee's Black-out book*, *The Shelter Book*, *The Brighter Black-Out Book* and *The Black–Out Book* by Evelyn August. These were compendia of articles, playlets, quizzes, puzzles and items of general interest designed to keep the family, and most importantly the children, occupied, and to take their minds off the imminent danger of air raids. They were 'the ideal companion for those long black-out evenings', as *The Black-Out Book*'s original cover blurb put it; 'the one hundred-and-one black-out nights' entertainment – A book you can safely give as a present to one friend or to an entire family.'

The early months of World War II became marked by a general lack of military activity in what was dubbed 'the phoney war'. Relief at the lack of enemy action was soon replaced by a growing tide of complaints against wartime measures introduced by the government, especially the black-out. Weeks of being confined to the house with the children, at a time of no television or no computer games, could result in the kind of clash so accurately depicted in the cartoon on page 53. One government minister commented that while the public were prepared for great sacrifices, they were not prepared for petty inconveniences. There were strident calls to 'Turn on the lights and turn out the ARP [Air Raid Precautions]', the Civil Defence services.

The spring of 1940 brought the phoney war to an end with the launch of the German 'blitzkrieg', lightening war, against western Europe. The fall of France in May 1940 meant that Britain was next, and that summer saw dog-fights over southern England as the might of the German Luftwaffe battled with the 'few' of the RAF for mastery of the skies over Britain in advance of an invasion.

Unable to defeat the RAF in open battle, the Luftwaffe turned its attention to Britain's cities in an attempt to destroy the country's morale. What became known as the 'Blitz' began on Saturday 7 September 1940 with a massive attack on London's docks by wave after wave of German bombers that lasted 11 hours and left over 430 dead and 1,600 injured.

Immediately all complaints about the black-out ceased while the ARP went from figures of derision to heroes. Now the cosy nights of the previous winter were put into perspective by nights spent in cold, drafty and damp 'Anderson' air raid shelters, crowded and unsanitary public street shelters, or places such as the London Underground where those still using the tube stepped over those sheltering on the platforms.

Keeping the children quiet during the hours spent 'under warning', especially in the tight confines of an Anderson shelter – 6ft-high, 4ft-6in wide, and 6ft-long (1.8m x 1.4m x 1.8m) – was an absolute necessity. Card games and board games were popular, as were books and comics of all sorts, and once again *The Black-Out Book* and its ilk became sought after. Whereas the children's Christmas gift of choice in 1939 had been very military in flavour – tin helmets and child-size army, navy, air force or Red Cross nurses' uniforms – such books were ideal gifts for Christmas 1940, spent, as often as not, in the air raid shelter.

Over the next few years, as shortages of raw materials really came into play, and ever fewer children's toys were produced, books such as *The Black-Out Book* became favourite possessions, studied and read repeatedly from cover to cover, until at last they were taken to the playground for 'swaps'. There they were highly-prized, or sold second-hand, where even dog-eared they could command higher prices than when new. Then they would once again be poured over and re-read until, inevitably, they began to fall to pieces, and patched beyond use, they would do one last service, joining the other scrap paper as part of the salvage drive.

The compiler of *The Black-Out Book*, Evelyn August, was actually the pen name of not one, but two extraordinary people; the married couple Sydney and Muriel Box. Sydney Box was born on 29 April 1907, in Beckenham, Kent, while Muriel was born Violette Muriel Baker in Tolworth, Surrey, on 22 September 1905. She tried her hand, unsuccessfully, at acting and dancing, before taking a job as a continuity girl for British International Pictures, becoming a script girl for director Anthony Asquith in the late 1920s.

Sydney was the eldest son of a nurseryman, and when his father joined the army in World War I, Sydney took on the role of head of the family. He began writing when, at the age of thirteen, he penned a weekly column for the *Kentish Times*. Leaving school at sixteen, he became a junior clerk, but continued to write his column, taking up a post on the local paper at seventeen, later becoming editor of the *Christian Herald* for three years.

Sydney and Muriel met in 1932, when he tried, unsuccessfully, to have a script accepted for a film. They married in May 1935, and in the following year their only daughter Leonora was born. This was Sydney's second marriage, having previously married the actress Katherine Knight in 1929, whom he had divorced four years later. By now Sydney was making a name for himself writing plays, and over the next few years he and Muriel wrote nearly forty of them together, while in 1935 they co-wrote the short detective film *Alibi Inn*, an unremarkable 'quickie' now lost in the mists of time.

Their plays were most successful, and by the late thirties they were earning a good living from their royalties, and from scriptwriting for the cinema. However with the outbreak of war all that changed; the government ordered the closure of cinemas, theatres and the like, as they were considered safety risks in the expected raids. Plays shut down, as did small film companies, and like many others Sydney and Muriel lost their jobs and their incomes. To compensate for this they put together *The Black-Out Book*, based largely on material Sydney had used in his articles for the *Christian Herald*. It was published in November 1939, and was immediately a great success, selling out within a few months.

In March 1940 Sydney formed the production company 'Verity Films' with Jay Gardner Lewis, to make short government propaganda and training films, including *The English Inn* in 1941, Muriel's first effort at directing.

Post-war, the Rank Organisation hired Sydney to head Gainsborough Pictures, and in 1945 he produced *The Seventh Veil*, which the couple scripted together, and for which they won the 1946 Oscar for best original screenplay. They continued to collaborate successfully into the 1950s, with Sydney producing and scripting, while Muriel co-produced some films including *The Man Within* and *Dear Murderer*, and co-scripted others, such as *The Girl in the Painting* and *Christopher Columbus*. In 1951, Sydney created 'London Independent Producers', which gave Muriel more opportunities to direct, a rare feat for a woman in what was then an industry almost entirely dominated by men. In 1958 Sydney ended his cinema work in order to concentrate on television production. Muriel continued to direct, up to her final film, *Rattle of a Simple Man*, in 1964. She went on to write novels and created a successful publishing house, Femina.

Sydney and Muriel divorced in 1969, and a year later Muriel married Gerald Gardiner, who had been Lord Chancellor. Sydney died on 25 May 1983 in Perth, Australia, while Muriel died in London on 19 May 1991.

ACKNOWLEDGMENTS

THE Publishers would like to thank the following for permission to include passages in this book.

Harper Collins for the Maurice Maeterlinck and Bertrand Russell extracts; PFD for the work of Eric Linklater; Stefan Lorant's estate for the extract from *I was Hitler's Prisoner*; and the family of Nancy Price for the inclusion of the passage from *The Gull's Way*.

PREFACE

THIS little book was planned with one purpose in mind—to provide the average family with sufficient amusement and entertainment for one hundred and one black-out nights. For that reason I flung the net wide and made the contents as varied as I knew how.

I think that probably nobody will enjoy every item in the book. I hope that nobody will fail to enjoy some. Among the five hundred and more items there are some intended mainly for adults and some mainly for children, but the great majority will appeal equally to either, and most adults—especially fathers—will insist in any case on sampling the items which were intended for the children.

There are more than a hundred problems and competitions, the answers to which you will find listed at the back of the book.

In conclusion, I should like to acknowledge my indebtedness to the many people who have so willingly given their assistance in the compilation of this volume, in particular to Muriel and Sydney Box (who gave me the use of all their " Strictly Personal " and " A—Zoo " rhymes), John Bourne, J. M. Sinclair, and most of all to John Woods, whose drawings, as they say in the catalogues, " speak for themselves."

E. A.

HERE BEGINNETH
THE
ONE-HUNDRED-AND-ONE
BLACK-OUT NIGHTS'
ENTERTAINMENT

Of all modern notions, the worst is this : that domesticity is dull. Inside the home, they say, is dead decorum and routine ; outside is adventure and variety. But the truth is that the home is the only place of liberty, the only spot on earth where a man can alter arrangements suddenly, make an experiment or indulge in a whim. The home is not the one tame place in a world of adventure ; it is the one wild place in a world of rules and set tasks.

G. K. Chesterton

The Sergeant counts his Men

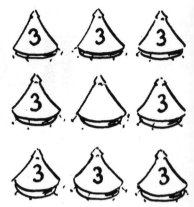

A RATHER illiterate sergeant was given charge of a party of twenty-four soldiers and told to see that none of them left camp during the night and that nobody entered the camp to see them. The camp consisted of nine tents, and the sergeant took the centre one for himself, putting three men in each of the remaining eight. To reassure himself that they were all present, he went round the tents and counted all of the men every quarter of an hour. After a while, he found that it was much easier to count up to nine along each row, arguing that so long as there were nine men in each row, there must be twenty-four altogether. One bright fellow heard the sergeant counting and realizing what he was doing, hit upon a scheme whereby four men slipped out and spent the evening in town without the sergeant noticing that they had gone. Late that night the four men came back bringing four friends with them, and later still four more of their cronies crept in to join them—yet the sergeant still counted nine in each row and was perfectly happy. How was it done ?

A—Zoo

No. 1. The Jaguar

When the male saw the female Jaguar
He said : " Good Heavens !   What
*   a haguar ! "*

The English . . .

It seems to me that extraordinary things are done in England, but they are all done to make money. The extraordinary thing in France is to spend money.

MONTESQUIEU (1721)

The English have no nerves.

CATHERINE II (1770)

Our own literature has sprung for the greater part from that of England. Our novels, our tragedies, where have they come from if not from Goldsmith, Fielding, and Shakespeare?

GOETHE (1822)

The English are the most practical race in the world.

REICHENSPERGER (1867)

"*Isn't this black-out dreadful? I simply cannot find my way about.*"

"*Never mind, dear, you'll soon be able to see in the dark like the other cats.*"

RATIONS

I HEARD it in the tube and train; I heard it in the bus; I saw it in the papers: "They've begun to ration us!" And I watched the people round me on work or pleasure bent. Some took it with a cheerful shrug and some with discontent. At first, I must admit, the prospect seemed a little glum, and then I reconsidered it, and found the time had come to count the many things I knew would never be 'cut down'—the kind of things we may forget through living in a town. You may not have the petrol to run a motor-car, but courage is a spirit that will get you just as far. You may not have the meat you want, the butter, or the tea, but the bread of human kindness always has, and will be, free. And if you're short of coal, don't worry—you can play your part. The fire of love can always be kept burning in your heart.

You can't black-

I stood and stared ; the sky was lit.
The sky was stars all over it.

RALPH HODGSON

IT may be an ill black-out, but, like the wind, it has brought some good things with it. For instance, it has started quite a few people looking at the stars—particularly those city-dwellers to whom starshine at night has hitherto meant nothing more than Greta Garbo, or the Guinness sign in Piccadilly Circus.

Now they are looking up and enjoying the experience, notwithstanding that crick in the neck afterwards.

Perhaps you are looking up yourself and wondering what it is all about ? If so, you will find on every other page of *The Black-out Book* a series of first-aids to star-gazing—little drawings like the one in the next column, enabling you to recognize the principal constellations.

For your general information, there are about 5000 ' fixed ' stars visible to the naked eye, but the number you can count on any one night will not be much greater than 1500. They are not really fixed at all, but travel through space at greater speeds than Eyston ever knew—200 miles a second, and that sort of thing.

A camera reveals about two

THE INFLUENCE OF MARS

I SLIPPED into the garden for a breath of cool night air, and on pausing for a moment, remained to stand and stare. For shimmering and glimmering above me in the sky a million twinkling stars held my fascinated eye. Somehow I hadn't realized their beauty until now—the Milky Way, the Dog-Star, the Great Bear, or the Plough—for everywhere around me not the faintest gleam of light was allowed to penetrate the velvet darkness of the night. And I thought it rather strange that the influence of Mars should be the means of showing us the loveliness of stars.

out the Stars !

million stars, and astronomers say that there must be fifty million altogether, but Woods has only drawn you two or three hundred —his wrist got tired after that. Most of them are as big as our sun—and the sun's nearly one and a half million times as large as the earth—so they are pretty big, really.

It takes at least four years for their light to reach the earth, so that by the time they hear of the black-out it will probably be too late for them to do anything about it. And then there is the Milky Way, or Galaxy, which has mil-

lions of stars of its own and is a thousand times as far away.

In ancient times star-gazers gave fanciful names to the principal constellations—the Babylonians tried their hand at it, and Ptolemy did a great deal of star-christening in the second century A.D. As these are still the best aids to remembering which group is which, Woods has incorporated in his drawings the outlines of the ancients' bears and snakes and heavenly twins.

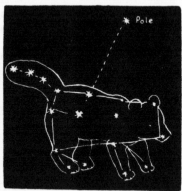

No. 1. Ursa Major
(the Great Bear)

THIS constellation is almost directly overhead in the spring. In the winter its position is a little to your right as you face

due north, but the best way to find it—and all the other constellations—is to begin by tracking down the Polar Star (*Stella Polaris*). You must realize that most of the stars visible to us in the Northern Hemisphere rise and set, so that the number which can be seen at any given time—and the position of each in the sky— varies with the hour and the season. The Great Bear's seven brightest stars suggest the shape of a ploughshare, and are known to many people as the Plough, Charles's Wain, the Chariot, or the Dipper. Dubhe and Merak (the Loins) are the pointers to the Pole Star. If you draw an imaginary line through them they will always lead you direct to *Stella Polaris*.

It's on the Tip of my Tongue!

THIS is where the entire family gets together with pencil and paper, while one trusted person assumes possession of the book and reads out the questions. In most cases a list of answers is given, and all you have to do is to spot the correct one. The right answers are at the back of the book. Now here goes—

1. Which of these substances can be made out of milk?

Ash-trays, balls, buttons, cheese, cloth, combs, cream, cups, ice-cream, paint.

2. By how much does the average person's hair grow each month?

⅛ inch, ¼ inch, ½ inch, 1 inch.

3. What is the number of bones in the human body?

164, 206, 270, 320.

4. Which of the following are musical instruments?

Psalm, psaltery, harmonica, hyperion, euphonium, euphonious, euphonicon, bassoon, bassinette, dictaphone.

5. How far does the average housewife walk on a normal day?

800 yards, 2 miles, 4 miles, 6 miles.

6. Who wrote " Lord of our far-flung battle-line " ? What is the name of the poem? And what is its first line?

7. There is one motor-car in Great Britain for every—

6 people, 12 people, 17 people, 28 people, 54 people.

8. What fraction of an inch is the diameter of a hair?

$$\frac{1}{1000}, \quad \frac{1}{500}, \quad \frac{1}{400}, \quad \frac{1}{100}, \quad \frac{1}{50}.$$

9. What is the number of players in a polo team?

2, 4, 5, 7.

A—Zoo

No. 2. The Polar Bear

What is this life if, full of care,
We have no time to stand and stare?
             W. H. DAVIES

Davies would like the Polar bear—
He has time to stand and stare.

Little Things

THERE never was a golden world, and I don't suppose there ever will be, yet every now and then—in moments of delight —we catch the glint and gleam of it. I don't mean lumps of colossal, glittering happiness, but moments brought about by little things. There's delight in ordinary city streets—the smell of roasting coffee alone might stop a desperate man from committing suicide. I once stood several minutes outside a fishmonger's in an ecstatic marine reverie, because I had caught sight of a noble, rich-looking fish, and it had set me thinking about the sea—all the oceans in the world, their vast extent, their strength

But you told me to get a luminous dial !

and mystery, the incredible variety of life in them.

J. B. PRIESTLEY

BOOKS

READ not to contradict and confute, nor to believe and take for granted, nor to find talk and discourse, but to weigh and consider. Some *Books* are to be tasted, others to be swallowed, and some few to be chewed and digested ; that is, some *Books* are to be read only in parts ; others to be read, but not curiously, and some few to be read wholly, and with diligence and attention. Some *Books* also may be read by deputy, and extracts made of them by others ; but that would be only in the less important arguments.

FRANCIS BACON

Strictly Personal

No. 1. Mr Ivor Novello

Hello, hello,
Mr Novello,
How are you doing up there at the Lane?

" I'm getting more mellow,"
Says Mr Novello,
" By doing it over and over again! "

You can't black-out the Stars

No. 2. Ursa Minor (the Little Bear)

The Little Bear is easy to find because almost at the tip of his tail is the Pole Star (*Stella Polaris*), which the Persians used to say "held all the constellations by the hand."

UNIFORMS

I WONDER if you've noticed as you go your varied ways, the number of fresh uniforms one sees about these days. Though every one is different in colour or in style, they have a common meaning, undeniably worth while— the service of their country in these times of strain and stress, when courage is demanded and true unselfishness. Yet there are many millions in this land of ours to-day who, though they wear no uniforms, serve in a quiet way. Their courage is unquestioned and their sense of duty clear. They face the future cheerfully, as though they knew no fear. At kitchen sinks they stand for hours : they wash, they cook, they sew. Their uniform's an apron—in case you didn't know !

Kiddicorner
SHADOWSNAPS

HERE'S a fascinating game which you can make for yourself.

It is probably one of the oldest games in the world, for it is said to have been invented by a Chinese named Tan, thousands of years B.C.

It consists of seven little geometrical figures which can be arranged to form amusing caricatures of animals and human beings. The shape of the pieces varies slightly in some versions of the game, but those illustrated here are the most usual.

To make them, mark out a 4-inch square of wood and cut it with a fretsaw into seven pieces exactly

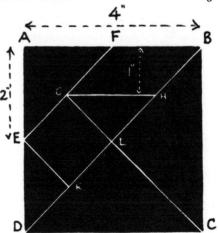

like those set out in the diagram. Stiff cardboard and a sharp penknife will do as substitutes if you are not a fretwork enthusiast.

Colour the pieces black on both sides, and you are all ready to begin making your own Shadowsnaps.

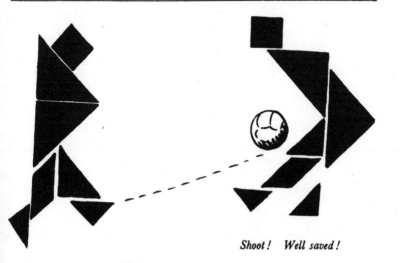

Shoot!   Well saved!

Animal Crackers

ALL the birds and beasts of this world have correct names for themselves, their friends, their families, and their homes.

How many of them do you know?

1. Give the correct name for the wife of each of the following :

    (a) Lion.
    (b) Tiger.
    (c) Wolf.
    (d) Stag.
    (e) Rooster.

2. Give the correct name for the husband of each of the following :

    (a) Sow.
    (b) Ewe.
    (c) Mare.
    (d) Goose.
    (e) Vixen.

3. Give the correct name for the baby of each of the following parents :

    (a) Elephant.
    (b) Fox.
    (c) Goose.
    (d) Swan.
    (e) Horse.

4. Give the correct name for a gathering of the following :

    (a) Mackerel.
    (b) Starlings.
    (c) Partridges.
    (d) Geese.
    (e) Sheep.

5. Give the correct name for the home of the following :

    (a) Cow.
    (b) Pigeon.
    (c) Beaver.
    (d) Sheep.
    (e) Eagle.

6. Give the correct name for the call of the following :

    (a) Cock.
    (b) Crow.
    (c) Donkey.
    (d) Owl.
    (e) Wolf.

A—Zoo

No. 3. The Stork

The refined Stork
Always uses a knife and fork.

The Trouble with Mottoes

A MAN said, "While I breathe, I hope," but no fish rose. So he turned the remark into Latin and tried again. And then everybody saw it was a splendid motto, and there was loud applause. *Dum spiro spero!* Put like that, it sounds good, and implies armorial bearings, sunlight through stained glass, and the great organ.

But the trouble with these mottoes and proverbs, whether in plain English or dressed for Sunday, is that they give us the block of concrete when our order is for a yard of elastic. They will not stretch. They make no allowance for the individual or the circumstances.

BARRY PAIN

Dye it black, please.

Black, *madam?*

Yes, my boy's an A.R.P. Warden, and he says he can't take me out because I contravene the black-out regulations.

PARIS

The Land of Cookery

GIVE Cartwright his Parliaments fresh each year,
But those friends of Short Commons would never do here;
And let Romilly speak as he will on the question,
No Digest of Law's like the laws of digestion!
Though many, I own, are the evils they've brought us,
Though Royalty's here on her very last legs,
Yet who can help loving the land that has taught us
Six hundred and eighty-five ways to dress eggs?

THOMAS MOORE

BEN BATTLE

BEN BATTLE was a soldier
   bold,
   And used to war's alarms ;
But a cannon ball took off his
   legs,
   So he laid down his arms.

Now as they bore him off the
   field,
   Said he, " Let others shoot,
For here I leave my second leg,
   And the Forty-Second Foot ! "

Now Ben he loved a pretty maid,
   Her name was Nelly Gray,
So he went to pay her his devours
   When he'd devoured his pay. . . .

Said she : " Before you had those
   timber toes
   Your love I did allow,
But then, you know, you stand upon
   Another footing now ! "

" Oh false and fickle Nellie Gray,
   I know why you refuse ;
Though I've no feet, some other
   man
   Is standing in my shoes. . . .

" Oh, Nellie Gray ! Oh, Nellie
   Gray !
   Is this your love so warm ?
The love that loves a scarlet coat
   Should be more uniform ! "

                              THOMAS HOOD

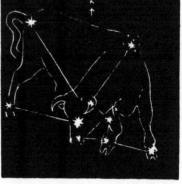

Strictly Personal

No. 2. Mr Winston Churchill

*Rule Britannia ? When Winston rules the
   waves,*
*The winds are still, and Neptune e'en
   behaves !*

You can't black-out the Stars

No. 3. *Taurus* (the Bull)

In the winter sky, Taurus hangs high
above the southern horizon, between
Aries and Gemini. The seven little
stars clustered to the right of it are
the Pleiades, or Seven Sisters.

Cut it Short!

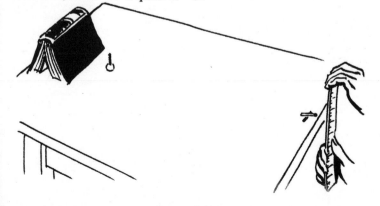

NEVER before in the history of mankind has the world been so full of initials. We are all of us in such a hurry that we can never find time to say " British Broadcasting Corporation "—it's so much quicker to say " B.B.C."

One result of this is that many of us forget what the initials really stand for. How many of you, for instance, can give the full names of the people or organizations which are usually referred to by the following initials?

1. M.C.C.
2. M.W.B.
3. M.R.C.S.
4. M.M.B.
5. L.C.C.
6. M.R.C.P.
7. B.O.B.
8. I.L.P.
9. I.R.A.
10. M.B.
11. M.P.
12. P.M.
13. P.M.G.
14. A.A.
15. A.A.A.

And finally, can you give three separate uses of the initials " P.C." ?

Kiddicorner

MARKSMANSHIP

Now, then, youngsters! Here's a way of testing your marksmanship.

Prop up a book at one end of the table. In front of it stand a match-stick, stuck in a piece of bread or plasticine. Now prop up one match across another at the other end of the table and, using a ruler, see how often you can hit the target with it.

Number, Please!

CAN you write down the same odd number five times, so that the five figures add up to 14?

Well, then, can you write down four nines so that they add up to 100?

Too easy? Then try adding together four fives to make 6½.

If your son comes to you and says: "In three years' time I shall be three times as old as I was three years ago," how old is your son?

A—Zoo

No. 4. The Rhinoceros

" I never play cricket," said the Rhinoceros,
" For I find that I always lose the tosseros! "

I remember . . .

ONCE when I was a boy I ran away from school, and late at night concluded to climb into the window of my father's office and sleep on a lounge, because I had a delicacy about going home and getting thrashed. As I lay there, and my eyes grew accustomed to the darkness, I fancied I could see a long, dusky, shapeless thing stretched out upon the floor.

A cold shiver went through me; I was afraid the thing would creep over and seize me in the dark. It seemed to me that the lagging moonlight would never, never get to it. I turned to the wall and counted twenty, to pass the feverish time away. I looked—the pale square of light was almost touching it.

With desperate will, I turned again and counted one hundred and faced about, all in a tremble. A white hand lay in the moonlight! Such an awful sinking at the heart—Such a gasp for breath. I counted again and looked—a naked arm was exposed. I put my hands over my eyes and counted until I could stand it no longer, and then—the pallid face of a man was there, with the corners of the mouth drawn down and the eyes fixed and glassy in death! I stared at the corpse till the light crept down to the bare breast—inch by inch—and disclosed a ghastly stab!

When I reached home, they whipped me, but I enjoyed it. That man had been stabbed that afternoon near the office, and they carried him in to doctor him, but he only lived an hour. I have slept in the same room with him often, since then—in my dreams.

MARK TWAIN

Laughter-pieces

Don't waste matches in a blackout ! Make them do two jobs—give you light when you need it and give you amusement when you have half an hour to spare.

Here's one way of using matches to provide you with entertainment, and you'll find plenty more in later pages.

The idea is to take as many matches as you can borrow from father—he's probably borrowed the household box already !—and arrange them to make caricatures, or designs, like those in the next column. They're not exactly masterpieces—but they are laughter-pieces. Can you improve on them ?

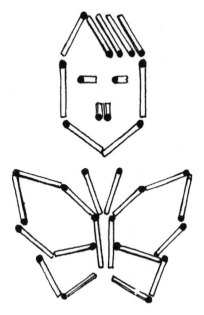

* * *

The Sunday-school teacher asked a little boy in her class :

" Who made you, Tommy ? "

" Well, God made part of me," said Tommy.

" What on earth do you mean?"

" Well," said Tommy, " I mean that God made me little and I growed the rest myself."

* * *

I never saw a Purple Cow—
I never hope to see one.
But I can tell you anyhow
I'd rather see than be one.
GELETT BURGESS

Patriotism

Can You write a Poem?

EVERY family has its own poet or poetess.

Most of them have more than one, for all of us have written poetry at one time or another.

Cousin Marjorie says the only difficulty about writing poetry is finding the rhymes. Do you agree? Because if you do, you're going to find this a delightfully easy game to play.

Every one has a slip of paper, and the person with the book reads out the list of rhymes. If he reads:

    lamb   went
    snow   go

you'll have no difficulty in converting that into "Mary had a little lamb."

You've got the idea? Very good! Let's see what you can do with these.

1. Soon   noon
   strong   long

2. socks   mocks
   ever   never

3. merry   after
   cherry   laughter

When you've done those, can you recognize the well-known poem which has the following rhymes in its second verse? (If you can't, you'll find it later in the book.)

    Sky   warp
    nigh   sharp
    forgot   not.

✖   ✖   ✖

Strictly Personal

No. 3. Noel Coward

(To the tune of "My Bonny lies over the Ocean.")

The young woman wept as she told us:
" I'm living in absolute hell!
The Navy has called up my husband
And taken dear Noel as well!

Bring back, bring back, Oh bring back
*   my Noel to me!*
Keep my husband, but bring back my
*   Noel to me!"*

You can't black-out the Stars

No. 4. Virgo

The chief beauty of the Virgin, which lies between Leo and Libra, is Spica (sometimes called the Ear of Corn), a fine white star almost of the first magnitude, which Woods has drawn at her left foot.

Statesmanship guyed

The efforts of statesmen have succeeded in completely maintaining collective insecurity.

In the interests of peace, energetic measures against the victims of aggression must be taken.

No sacrifice made by others is too much for the cause of peace.

The Czechs have not been sold out—just given away for nothing.

Treaties are made to be kept by the weaker nation.

Localizing a conflict means leaving the victim to his fate.

There are many who like to warm their soup over a conflagration.

KAREL CAPEK

SANDBAGS

THEY started in the morning ; they've been going on all day, shovelling up the sand to fill the bags they drag away to pile against the windows of shop, and house, and store. Somehow it didn't seem the thing that sand was destined for. I thought of little Rosemary, in Sussex by the sea, building golden castles and patting them with glee. I thought of camels winding across the desert waste, towards a green oasis without a sign of haste. And then came the thought that I couldn't turn away, of the hour-glass that measures life with sand, day by day.

The Fair Farmer

THIS problem is so simple that you'll probably see through it at once — if not sooner!

It's about a farmer who was reputed to be a very fair man. He owned a large tract of land, only a quarter of which was more than sufficient for his own needs.

He decided, therefore, to give the remainder of the land to his four sons. Bearing in mind his reputation for fairness, he resolved that each son should have a portion of exactly the same area and shape.

How did he manage this?

At the Mid-Hour of Night

At the mid-hour of night, when stars are weeping, I fly
To the lone vale we loved, when life shone warm in thine eye ;
And I think oft, if spirits can steal from the regions of air
To revisit past scenes of delight, thou wilt come to me there,
And tell me our love is remember'd even in the sky.

Then I sing the wild song it once was rapture to hear,
When our voices commingling breathed like one on the ear ;
And as Echo far off through the vale my sad orison rolls,
I think, O my love ! 'tis thy voice from the Kingdom of Souls
Faintly answering still the notes that once were so dear.

THOMAS MOORE

Mr Middleton's Garden

THIS is a good game to play when you and the children have been listening to Mr Middleton broadcasting—or when Father has been going through the seed catalogues ordering next year's supplies for the garden.

One player begins : " Mr Middleton's garden is a fine garden, because it contains (say) fuchsias." Then all of the other players must follow with the same sentence, but substitute a different flower, beginning with the same letter. (So don't say " phlox," even if it does sound the same !)

If you are in doubt about any of the words put forward by one of the players, consult a dictionary, or, if you prefer it, Mr Middleton.

A—Zoo

No. 5. The Seal

A Seal is something you put on a letter.

THE MARX BROTHERS

Formula for Success

IF you want to be successful in life, there's a simple algebraical formula you should follow.

At least, that is what Professor Einstein says.

He told an inquirer :

" Let A equal success in life, let X equal hard work, and let Y equal exercise and play. Got that ? Good ! Then $X+Y+Z$ will equal A."

" But what is Z ? " he was asked.

" That," he answered, " is keeping your mouth shut ! "

" *What's happened to your balloon, young man ?* "

" *Must have done the Indian rope-trick, lady.*"

TAKE YOUR CHOICE?

IN each of the statements made below there is a gap where the essential information should be. Fill that gap from the alternatives listed under each. The correct answers· are at the end of the book.

1. In Britain there is one civil servant to every —— people.

102, 316, 437, 964, 1060.

2. In Britain there is one judge to every —— people.

100,000, 200,000, 300,000, 500,000.

3. *Vanity Fair* was written by ——.

George Meredith, Jane Austen, William Thackeray, Charles Dickens, Laurence Sterne.

4. A racing motorist reaches the peak of his ability at the age of ——.

20, 23, 28, 31, 40.

5. There are approximately —— kinds of insects known to science.

2,500, 14,000, 100,000, 750,000.

6. The number of radio licences issued in Britain is more than ——.

7 million, 8 million, 9 million.

7. Red-headed people are usually —— intelligent than the average.

more, less.

8. About —— per cent. of the earth's surface is covered by water.

15, 27, 34, 51, 72, 80.

9. The sun is —— than most of the other stars.

larger, smaller.

10. The population of the world is estimated to be —— millions.

801, 937, 1164, 1780, 2134.

You can't black-out the Stars

No. 5. *Scorpio* (the Scorpion)

Scorpio lies between Libra and Sagittarius and is at its best in the summer, when it hangs close to the south-west horizon, below the Milky Way. Antares, its biggest star, is known as the Eastern Beacon.

How Many Fathers?

HERE'S a problem for every father's son—and for every son's father!

In a certain street, one-fifth of the fathers were Territorials, one-third were doing A.R.P. work of one sort or another, three times the difference between these two groups were too old for National Service, and one was a pilot in the Royal Air Force. How many fathers were there altogether?

* * *

If you've managed to solve that, here's another paternal problem:

A father went into a shop to buy a birthday present for his son. While it was being wrapped up, he remarked to the assistant: "You know, if I were two years older, I should be exactly three times as old as the boy—but in eight years' time I'll only be twice as old as he is."

How old are father and son now?

Strictly Personal

No. 4. Sir Seymour Hicks

Some old dogs can learn new tricks—
Pray regard Sir Seymour Hicks,
Reappearing to commence a
War-time job as head of Ensa.

THE SENTRY

A FIGURE loomed before me in the dusk as I went home. It was the guard on duty outside the aerodrome. He stood, a silent sentry, with his bayonet upright, impassive but impressive in the strange half-light. I wondered, as I left him to his lonely vigil there, how many things we fail to guard because we do not care: our lips when they would utter words of anger or of spite; our eyes when they would countenance deceit, however slight; our ears when they would listen to the slander of a friend—we should always be on duty, like a sentry, to the end.

Come to a Full Stop!

IF Father ever complains that his typist punctuates his letters badly, get him to try his hand at this.

It's just a simple series of sentences from which the punctuation has been omitted. All Father—or any other victim you select—has to do is to read it aloud at normal speed, so that it makes sense. It's quite easy, really ! Just come to a full stop at the right places and there you are.

Walking along a street in a black-out may produce some strange adventures if you suffer from flat feet you should try standing on your toes holding the breath is recommended as a cure for hiccoughs when there is no poison in the house children and pets are safe from the danger of frost-bite there is no protection save warmth and good circulation like newspapers magazines have articles columns pictures and print tigers are animals but mosquitoes are insects like flies in a theatre wings are used for storing scenery what is to be must be say the Arabs when they ride scooters children should be careful not to open your mouth when a dentist asks you to is a sign of fear like father like son is a wise saying such things as knives and forks are dangerous for very small children with umbrellas and mackintoshes people trudge through the rain looking for the kerb is the most difficult part of the black-out.

(In case you're still doubtful, the sentences end at the following words : adventures, toes, hiccoughs, safe, circulation, print, insects, scenery, Arabs, careful, fear, saying, children, rain, black-out.)

———

A—Zoo

No. 6. The Giraffe

Whenever I see a Giraffe
I want to laugh.

" You wait ! I'll—I'll drop a leaflet on you ! "

Don't waste Matches !

Here's a match problem for you to match your wits against.

Take seventeen ordinary matches and arrange them in a design like this.

How many squares are there in the design ?

Can you take away two matches and leave half as many ?

Frankenstein

THIS fascinating story is taken from *Wilderness Wife*, by Kathrene Pinkerton—the story of a city girl who went to live in the Canadian backwoods :

On a portage one evening after blueberry-picking, we met Ash-wan-a-mak, an aged Indian, and his wife. We were surprised to find this feeble couple so far from their lake. Obviously they were worried. As the story came out, we strove desperately to keep our faces straight. Ash-wan-a-mak and his wife had taken a bear cub for a pet. It slept in their wigwam. But the bear grew to full size, took up most of the space beside the fire and became so strong the frail old couple could not control him. Often he ate all their food. As they expressed it, " The bear he got to be boss."

Ash-wan-a-mak could not bring himself to kill the bear, and at last in desperation they had run away from it. While they were still telling the story, the old Indian woman began a warning ' teckh,' and both stiffened. Then we heard a rustle in the brush, and out came a huge black bear.

He rushed up to the old couple and began nosing about for food. We went on at once, for the bear showed an interest in our packs. As we paddled around the next bend we looked back to see the reunited but disconsolate family.

CONJURING IN

CONJURING in the black-out! That should be very easy, shouldn't it? Well, so are most of the tricks on this page, although, of course, they *are* intended to be done with the lights on.

Swallowing a Table Knife

This trick should be performed while sitting at table. Take an ordinary table-knife and make several flourishes with it, pointing out how sharp it is, and so on. Then hold it in front of you, with both hands, the fingers entirely hiding the knife from the view of the audience. Make a few more flourishes, during one of which you drop the knife into your lap —but keep your hands rigid, as though the knife were still there. Then bring your hands together, as if you were breaking the knife in half, and pretend to push it into your mouth. To mystify the audience still more, demonstrate that you have nothing up your sleeves. But don't do this trick twice for the same people—the second time they'll spot how it's done.

The Magic Matches

Hold two ' book ' matches side

by side between your finger and thumb. (They should be wedged with the heads against your index finger and the other ends against your thumb.) Point out to the audience that they both have the maker's name printed on them. Then take them with the first finger and thumb of the other hand, turn them round, and demonstrate that on the reverse side they are plain. Do this several times, showing printed and plain sides alternatively. Then suddenly twist the matches between your fingers as you turn them, and you can produce a printed side over and over again at will. This is an extremely simple trick, but properly performed, it is very effective.

Sewing the Fingers Together

This illusion is one which can be performed by anyone with a certain gift for pantomime, and which will be found to amuse audiences of all ages. It was first shown to me by a German refugee several years ago, but since then it has been performed by such artists as Gene Sheldon and Max Wall.

First select a hair from your own head or that of your victim and pretend to pull it out. Then go through the motions of

THE BLACK-OUT

There are four of them altogether, and they can all be performed with a little practice and a lot of self-confidence, no special sleight of hand or fancy costume—and, best of all, no expense.

MAGIC WORDS

IF you're going to do any conjuring at all, you'll need a magic incantation to use at the required moments—and a constant flow of chatter (generally called by the professional ' patter '). The patter must be your own affair. The magic phrase most generally used is :

Abracadabra

This is supposed to date back to Assyrian times when the use of the word was actually recommended as an antidote for toothache; to be effective, however, it had to be written on a piece of parchment suspended from the neck in the following form :

```
ABRACADABRA
 ABRACADABR
  ABRACADAB
   ABRACADA
    ABRACAD
     ABRACA
      ABRAC
       ABRA
        ABR
         AB
          A
```

straightening the hair and threading it through a needle. Take this (non-existent) needle and pretend to push it through your little finger, drawing the ' thread ' through after it. Do the same with each of the other fingers in turn and then, with a special effort, the thumb. As the ' thread ' is pulled through each time, close the fingers as though they were being drawn together, and assume an agonized expression.

The Broken Nose Trick

This is another gruesome little trick, beloved of all schoolboys who see it. Hold the nose firmly in both hands and pretend to move it to and fro from right to left. The position of your hands should conceal the fact that your two thumbnails are tucked away against the front teeth of your upper jaw. Now, as you move your nose from side to side, you click the thumbnails against your teeth, with a delicious sound of cracking bone.

(You will find some more difficult tricks in a later page of this book.)

Blow, blow, thou Winter Wind!

Blow, blow, thou winter wind,
    Thou art not so unkind
    As man's ingratitude ;
Thy tooth is not so keen,
Because thou art not seen,
    Although thy breath be rude.

Heigh ho ! sing, heigh ho ! unto
    the green holly :
Most friendship is feigning, most
    loving mere folly :
    Then heigh ho, the holly !
    This life is most jolly.

Freeze, freeze, thou bitter sky,
That dost not bite so nigh
    As benefits forgot :
Though thou the waters warp,
Thy sting is not so sharp
    As friend remembered not.

Heigh ho ! sing, heigh ho ! unto
    the green holly :
Most friendship is feigning, most
    loving mere folly :
    Then heigh ho, the holly !
    This life is most jolly.
                    WILLIAM SHAKESPEARE

(*This is the poem referred to in the
problem for the Eighth Evening.*)

In the Dark

Two Air-Raid Wardens sat in their report post one dark night. One Air-Raid Warden was the father of the other Air-Raid Warden's son. What relation were they to each other ?

A twelve horse-power motor-car was driven down to Brighton—this was just before petrol rationing came in—with two fathers, two mothers, two sisters, two brothers, two daughters, two uncles and two aunts inside. Yet the car could only just hold six people. How do you explain it ?

Strictly Personal
No. 5. Beverley Nichols

*Ev'ry little flower that grows
Looks at Beverley and knows
That it's worth a line or two
In the Maestro's new Revue.*

Two
Ovens

HAVE you tried making word squares?

Here is a fairly easy example to start you off.

Below you will find a square

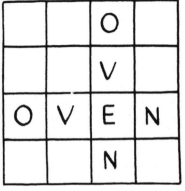

with the word OVEN filled in horizontally and vertically.

Using the letters of the following words:

LET
RED
TOP

fill in the square, so that it consists of nine complete words—four vertical, four horizontal, and one diagonally from top left to bottom right.

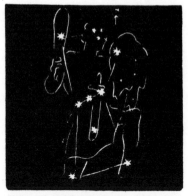

You can't black-out the Stars
No. 6. Orion

The most brilliant of the equatorial constellations and, after Ursa Major, the most familiar, Orion is the great glory of the winter heavens. In January it hangs in the centre of the southern sky. Betelgeuse and Rigel (the club and the left foot) are the brightest of its stars, while the three making up the belt are all double. These are sometimes called the Three Kings, since they are supposed to point to Sirius, the Star of Bethlehem.

If she will, she will, you may depend on't;
If she won't, she won't—and there's an end on't.

(From a Pillar in the Dane John Field, Canterbury.)

Spelling Bee

ONE of the oldest of games, and still one of the best, is the spelling bee. Mothers and fathers probably played it as children ; children have learned it lately from the B.B.C.

There are two ways of holding a spelling bee at home. One is for Father, or Mother, or some other responsible person, to read out a list of words and for each of the contestants to write down his idea of the correct spelling. A time-limit of not more than one minute per word should be imposed.

For larger parties, two sides can be picked, and each side can fire its carefully chosen words at the other. This is probably more fun, since it involves choosing difficult words, as well as spelling them. Here, too, a time-limit should be imposed — and all doubts about the correct spelling of words should be settled by consulting a dictionary.

Here are two groups of words which may be used for either type of contest :

GROUP ONE

Emphatic	Rheumatic
Parallelogram	Nucleus
Resinous	Trilogy
Filament	Pseudonym
Sequestered	Inertia
Bibulous	Taffrail
Modulate	Numerical
Counterfeit	

GROUP TWO

Hieroglyphic	Luscious
Irreducible	Pneumonia
Magnanimity	Dissociate
Hydraulic	Oleaginous
Pleurisy	Hyperbole
Iridescence	Lackadaisical
Jocose	Diphtheria
Genealogy	

" I don't care if you are going out with the Major, you can't do that ! "

Don't waste Matches!

Here are sixteen matches arranged in the shape of a diamond. How many triangles do they make?

Can you reduce that number to four by taking away four matches only?

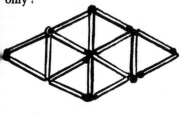

Every one is as God made him, and very often worse.

SANCHO PANZA'S PROVERBS

A—Zoo

No. 7. The Ostrich

*Did you ever see an Ostrich
Doing cross-stitch?*

I saw the Wind

TO see the wind, with a man his eyes, it is unpossible, the nature of it is so fine, and subtle, yet this experience of the wind had I once myself, and that was in the great snow that fell four years ago : I rode in the highway, the way being somewhat trodden afore by wayfaring men. The fields on both sides were plain and lay almost yard deep with snow, the night afore had been a little frost, so that the snow was hard and crusted above. That morning the sun shone bright and clear, the wind was whistling aloft, and sharp according to the time of the year. The snow in the highway lay loose and trodden with horse feet : so as the wind blew, it took the loose snow with it, and made it so slide upon the snow in the field which was hard and crusted by reason of the frost overnight, that thereby I might see very well, the whole nature of the wind as it blew that day. And I had a great delight and pleasure to mark it, which maketh me now far better to remember it. Sometime the wind would be not past two yards broad, and so it would carry the snow as far as I could see. Another time the snow would blow over half the field at once. Sometime the snow would tumble softly, by and by it would fly wonderfull fast. And this I perceived also that the wind goeth by streams and not whole altogether.   ROGER ASCHAM

Are You Afraid of the Dark ?

WE are all of us a little inclined to laugh at a child who admits to being frightened of the dark, but this is one of mankind's oldest fears, and most of us have some trace of it in our own make-up.

Truthfully, now—are *you* afraid of the dark ?

You're not sure ? Well, here's a way of finding out. Answer all of the following questions with absolute truth. Then consult the key at the bottom of the page, add up your score, and you'll know the answer !

1. Do you like to sit in the gloaming without the lamps lit ? (If it gives you a ' creepy ' feeling, answer ' No.')

2. Can you go to sleep without a light in your room ?

3. When you walk upstairs in the darkness, do you always feel sure that there is one more stair than there actually is ?

4. When you enter a darkened building which you have every reason to believe empty, do you suddenly feel sure that there is some one inside ?

5. When you walk down a deserted street at night, do you hear imaginary footsteps behind you ?

6. When you move about your own house in the dark, do you keep close to the walls and grip the banisters tightly ?

7. When you enter a cinema during the performance, do you slide your feet along the floor in case there should be steps you haven't noticed ?

8. Are you afraid to go to the coal-shed or garage in the garden after dark without a pocket torch ?

Now for the scores. Give yourself five marks for each answer which corresponds with the following : 1. Yes ; 2. Yes ; 3. No ; 4. No ; 5. No ; 6. No ; 7. No ; 8. No.

If your total is over 30, you are over-confident. From 15 to 30 is a sensible average, 10 indicates that you are slightly nervous, and less than 10 means that you are definitely frightened of the dark !

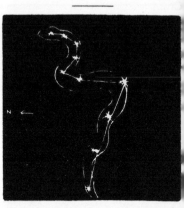

You can't black-out the Stars

No. 7. Serpens (the Serpent)

Just below the Northern Crown and between the Virgin and the Serpent-bearer is the Serpent, a constellation at its brightest in the spring.

Is This how You feel in the Dark?

BUT after innumerable fluttering thoughts, terrified to the last degree, looking behind me at every two or three steps, mistaking every bush and tree, and fancying every stump at a distance to be a man ; nor is it possible to describe how many various shapes affrighted imagination represented things to me in, how many wild ideas were found every moment in my fancy, and what strange, unaccountable whimsies came into my thoughts by the way. When I came to my castle, for so I think I called it ever after this, I fled into it like one pursued. . . .

ROBINSON CRUSOE

(That was written by Daniel Defoe, describing Robinson Crusoe's feelings when he saw Man Friday's footprint for the first time.)

Strictly Personal

No. 6. Dame Marie Tempest

A STORM IN A TEACUP

Tempest means storm—ask any sage—
Accompanied by rain and squalls,
But Marie's tempests only rage
Within the teacups in the stalls.

SLIPPERS

LOOK at his old brown slippers toasting in the fender, there ! They clutter up the fireplace, but no one's going to care. They aren't the least bit elegant and certainly not new, but a slipper should be comfortable, not stylish like a shoe. They look as though they're listening as they lie there in the hearth, for those old familiar footsteps coming up the garden path. He'll put them on and sigh and say : "It's lovely to be home," and stretch his feet before the fire and let his fancy roam. The troubles and the worries of the day are quickly gone, for there's nothing like old slippers, when all is said and done.

A—Zoo

No. 8. The Monkey
The average Monkey
Would hate to be a flunkey.

Kiddicorner

This Cat had Nine Lives

EVERY ONE knows that a cat has nine lives, but it's not often that we have the chance of seeing all nine lives lived in front of us.

But that is what happens in the little passage printed below. Every dash represents a word beginning with 'cat' and if you're really clever, you'll be able to find all nine without looking at the answers :

Tommy stopped shooting with his — because he saw his friend — coming along the road. She had been to service at the —, where she had recited her —. She was a —, but Tommy was hardly in the same —. As they passed his shop, the —, who was looking at a —, gave Tommy a length of — for his violin.

MILEAGE

A THOUGHT FOR THE PETROL-RATIONED MOTORIST

WHEN all is said, there is probably no vehicle that gives you so much mileage as your feet.

Feet are adjusted to our whole mechanism of sensation, of thought, and of feeling. They go just about fast enough to let you take in the whole scene without strain. They carry you along on a level with other men and above the heads of most animals —which is as it should be. They do not hold you so high that you cannot stoop to pick a flower or a strawberry.

Anyone who walks over ground which he customarily covers by motor-car will have the sensation one has when one sees a familiar article through a microscope. Every square yard of space has a thousand times as many things in it. Everything is clearer, sharper, rounder, and yet more mysteriously interesting.

To walk into the rain or the snow, to beat against the wind, is in itself to go somewhere, for rain and snow and wind make each its own world, and to him who fronts them bravely the elements are always kindly. Each sends him back to the tepid climate of his indoor world with its own gift in his spirit—with the peace of the falling snow on his heart, or the wild force of the wind in his purposes.

MARJORIE BARSTOW GREENBIE
in *The Arts of Leisure*

The Diamond and the Square

FIVE words, varying from one to seven letters in length, can be filled in on this diamond so that it will read the same across and down. Clues to each word are given below.

```
        x
      x x x
    x x x x x
  x x x x x x x
    x x x x x
      x x x
        x
```

1. A letter of the alphabet. 2. Cut. 3. A tooth. 4. An officer. 5. Diminished. 6. A colour. 7. A letter of the alphabet.

Now here's a word square which you should be able to solve very easily.

```
B x x x x
x L x x x
x x A x x
x x x C x
x x x x K
```

Reading from the top to bottom, the words making up the square are : 1. Empty. 2. Warning. 3. To meet in opposition. 4. Spot. 5. The part of a rope that hangs loose.

The correct solution must have five L's and five A's adjoining one another.

" What is the meaning of that A.R.P. on your car ? "

" Why, didn't you know, officer ? My boy friend put it there—it means A Real Peach."

Don't waste Matches !

Arrange 24 matches to make a design like this.

How many squares are there in the design ?

Now, by taking away 8 matches only, can you reduce the number of squares to two ?

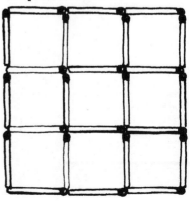

As Bald as a — ?

YOU'VE all heard of the man who was as dead as a door-nail, but have you ever stopped to consider how many similes like this we use in ordinary conversation ?

Here's a little game you can play *en famille* or by yourself. It's called

SILLY SIMILES

and the idea is to provide the recognized simile required to complete each of the following sentences. If you have any difficulty, turn to the end of the book and you'll find that it'll be as clear as crystal. (Sorry !) Now, here goes !

1. Bald as ——
2. Black as ——
3. Tight as ——
4. Weak as ——
5. Old as ——
6. Good as ——
7. Sly as ——
8. Heavy as ——
9. Brown as ——
10. Free as ——
11. Playful as ——
12. Dark as ——
13. Stiff as ——
14. Vain as ——
15. Plain as ——
16. Blind as ——
17. Cold as ——
18. Cool as ——
19. Hard as ——
20. Limp as ——

When you've guessed all those, you might try inventing a few yourself, with modern applications. For instance, " As easy as A B C " might read " As easy as A Bradman Century." And you might even coin a few phrases like " As horrific as Hitler ! "

Strictly Personal

No. 7. *Miss Deanna Durbin*

We like to listen when Miss Durbin
  Is singing at the grand pianna—
The only person she's disturbin'
  Is Miss Grace Moore—go on,
    Deanna !

It All depends Where You put Them!

Ten lumps of sugar—if you still have any, now that rationing's come in !—or ten nuts, or ten coins provide all the properties you need for this little problem.

Line them up in pairs and you have five rows, with two in a row, like this—

x x x x x
x x x x x

Now can you rearrange them, so that they form five rows with four in each row ?

What's that ? Ten into twenty won't go ? Oh, yes, it will ! And it's quite easy—when you know how !

On a Fly drinking out of His Cup

BUSY, curious, thirsty fly !
Drink with me and drink as I :
Freely welcome to my cup,
Could'st thou sip and sip it up :
Make the most of life you may,
Life is short and wears away.

Both alike are mine and thine,
Hastening quick to their decline :
Thine's a summer, mine's no more,
Though repeated to threescore.
Threescore summers, when they're gone,
Will appear as short as one !

WILLIAM OLDYS

You can't black-out the Stars

No. 8. Gemini (the Twins)

The Twins lie between Cancer and Taurus and to the east of the Great Bear. The two bright stars of this constellation are Castor and Pollux, the heavenly twins, sons of Jupiter and Leda, about whom you have probably read in mythology.

How It feels to retire

FOR the first day or two I felt stunned, overwhelmed. I could only apprehend my felicity ; I was too confused to taste it sincerely. I wandered about, thinking I was happy, and knowing that I was not. I was in the condition of a prisoner in the old Bastile, suddenly let loose after a forty years' confinement. I could scarce trust myself with myself. It was like passing out of Time into Eternity—for it is a sort of Eternity for a man to have his Time all to himself. It seemed to me that I had more time on my hands than I could ever manage. From a poor man, poor in Time, I was suddenly lifted up into a vast revenue ; I could see no end of my possessions; I wanted some steward, or judicious bailiff, to manage my estates in Time for me. And here let me caution persons grown old in active business, not lightly, nor without weighing their own resources, to forego their customary employment all at once, for there may be danger in it. I feel it by myself, but I know that my resources are sufficient ;

and now that those first giddy raptures have subsided, I have a quiet home-feeling of the blessedness of my condition. I am in no hurry. Having all holidays, I am as though I had none. If Time hung heavy upon me, I could walk it away ; but I do *not* walk all day long, as I used to do in those old transient holidays, thirty miles a day, to make the most of them. If Time were troublesome, I could read it away, but I do *not* read in that violent measure, with which, having no Time my own but candle-light Time, I used to weary out my head and eyesight in by-gone winters. I walk, read, or scribble (as now) just when the fit seizes me. I no longer hunt after pleasure ; I let it come to me. I am like the man—

> *That's born, and has his years*
> *come to him,*
> *In some green desert.*

" I have done all that I came into this world to do. I have worked task work and have the rest of the day to myself."

CHARLES LAMB

A—Zoo

No. 9. The Whale

The weeping Whale just cries and cries.
He'll be nothing but blubber till he dies.

Gentlemen, Please !

IT is almost the definition of a gentleman to say he is one who never inflicts pain. He makes light of favours while he does them and seems to be receiving when he is conferring.

He observes the maxim of the ancient sage, that we should ever conduct ourselves toward our enemy as if he were one day to be our friend.

CARDINAL NEWMAN

* * *

A gentleman is never rude, except intentionally.

" What are the trenches like in the winter, mate ? "
" Awful ! Mud up to your neck ! "
" Bli'me ! Whose neck ? "

Kiddicorner

The Geometrical Uncle

BOBBY was very interested in geometry—and so was his Uncle. They often used to talk about it, and Bobby was not at all surprised when one day his Uncle asked him to purchase the following :

Three-quarters of plus.
A circle.
A straight line and two semicircles.
A triangle on two feet.
Two semicircles.
Another circle.

Can you work out what it was Bobby's Uncle wanted ?

Football in the Black-out

WHAT I miss most in wartime," said Marjorie's young man, " is the football league matches. Football isn't football any more. . . ."

" Ever play black-out football ? " inquired Father.

" No. What's that ? " asked Marjorie's fiancé.

" Come on. I'll show you," said Dad.

And this is what he did.

First, to the accompaniment of muffled protests from Mother, he stuck two pins into each end of the old dining-room table, each pair being five inches apart.

" Those are the goal-posts," he observed. Then he produced two pennies and a sixpence. One penny he turned face upward, the other face downward, in order to distinguish between them.

" There," he said. " You take the head, and I'll take the tail. Now we can play football by taking turns to flick our own penny at the ball. Get the idea ? The penny hits the sixpence and it skims along just like a football.

Oh ! Good shot ! Goal to Herbert ! "

" Rather like shove-ha'penny, isn't it ? " observed Herbert, as they put the coins in the centre of the table, facing each other, and ' kicked off ' again.

There are variations of this game you can work out for yourselves—such as having two or three pennies a side and positioning them cleverly to stop

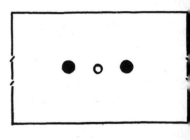

your opponents' attacks. In this variation, only one man may be moved at a time, of course.

A friend of mine has devised a game of black-out billiards in much the same way, but this calls for a rim round the table. By the way, if Mother objects to your using the dining-room table, that old wooden one in the kitchen or Dad's den will do just as well.

You can't black-out the Stars

No. 9. *Cancer* (the Crab)

Between Leo and Gemini you will find the Crab. That cluster of little stars it contains is known as Praesepe (the Beehive).

Strictly Personal

No. 8. *Clark Gable*

We can't help liking dear Clark Gable,
He acts as well as he is able.

LULLABY

SOFTLY sleep, my little
    one ;
  Cry no more, my love.
Life for you has just begun.
  Sleep, my pretty dove.

Close your bonny eyes for
    me,
  Slumber on and smile—
Blissful in security,
  Slumber on a-while.

Love created you, my sweet,
  Delicate and fair—
Dimpled hands and dimpled
    feet,
  Dimples everywhere.

Gently dream the hours
    away,
  Innocent of fear.
Till the dawn lets in the day
  Dream, my darling dear.

          MURIEL BOX

PRAYERS OF

Robert Herrick

Here a little child I stand,
Heaving up my either hand ;
Cold as Paddocks though they be,
Here I lift them up to Thee,
For a Benizon to fall
On our meat, and on us all.

 Amen.

* * *

God ! to my little meale and oyle,
Add but a bit of flesh, to boyle :
And Thou my Pipkinnet shalt see,
Give a *wave-offring* unto Thee.

* * *

Samuel Taylor Coleridge

He prayeth best who loveth best
 All things both great and
 small ;
For the dear God who loveth us,
 He made and loveth all.

* * *

John Bunyan

The Lord is only my support,
 And He that doth me feed ;
How can I then want any thing
 Whereof I stand in need ?

Henry VIII

Lord God, maker of all things,
we pray Thee now in this evening
hour to defend us through Thy
mercy from all deceit of our enemy.
Let us not be deluded with
dreams, but if we lie awake keep
Thou our hearts. Grant this
petition, O Father, for the sake
of Thy Son, to whom with Thee
and the Holy Ghost always in
heaven and earth be all laud and
honour.

* * *

Sir Walter Raleigh

E'en such is Time, which takes
 in trust
Our youth, our joys, our all we
 have . . .
Which in the dark and silent
 grave—
When we have wandered all our
 ways—
Shuts up the story of our days ;
And from which grave and earth
 and dust,
The Lord shall raise me up, I
 trust.

(Written the night before his execu-
tion, and found in his Bible in the
Gatehouse at Westminster.)

* * *

Robert Burns

Some have meat, and cannot eat,
Some would eat that want it ;
We have meat, and we can eat,
And so the Lord be thankit.

THE GREAT

Lady Jane Grey

O merciful God, be Thou now unto me a strong tower of defence, I humbly entreat Thee. Give me grace to await Thy leisure, and patiently to bear what Thou doest unto me ; nothing doubting or mistrusting Thy goodness towards me ; for Thou knowest what is good for me better than I do. Therefore do with me in all things what Thou wilt ; only arm me, I beseech Thee, with Thine armour, that I may stand fast ; above all things, taking to me the shield of faith ; praying always that I may refer myself wholly to Thy will, abiding Thy pleasure, and comforting myself in those troubles which it shall please Thee to send me, seeing such troubles are profitable for me ; and I am assuredly persuaded that all Thou doest cannot but be well ; and unto Thee be all honour and glory.

* * *

Plato

Lord of Lords, grant us the good, whether we pray for it or not, but evil keep from us, even though we pray for it.

William Blake

To Mercy, Pity, Peace, and Love
  All pray in their distress ;
And to these virtues of delight
  Return their thankfulness.

For Mercy, Pity, Peace, and Love
  Is God, our Father dear,
And Mercy, Pity, Peace, and Love
  Is Man, His child and care.

For Mercy has a human heart,
  Pity a human face,
And Love, the human form
    divine,
And Peace, the human dress.

Then every man, of every clime,
  That prays in his distress,
Prays to the human form divine,
  Love, Mercy, Pity, Peace.

And all must love the human
    form,
  In heathen, Turk, or Jew ;
When Mercy, Love, and Pity
    dwell
  There God is dwelling too.

JEWELS OF SUPERSTITION

MOST of us are fond of jewels—mainly, I suspect, because of the amount of money they represent—but the ancients surrounded them with superstitions of all kinds, many of which are still taken notice of by some people.

The most common of these are the supposition that each month of the year is under the influence of one particular stone. Unfortunately there are different ideas about which stone applies to which month, but the most generally accepted list, for those who are interested in such things, is :

January .	. Garnet .	. Constancy
February .	. Amethyst .	. Sincerity
March .	. Bloodstone .	. Courage
April .	. Diamond .	. Innocence
May . .	. Emerald .	. Love
June .	. Agate .	. Health
July .	. Cornelian .	. Content
August :	. Sardonyx .	. Married bliss
September .	. Chrysolite .	. Sanity
October .	. Opal .	. Hope
November .	. Topaz .	. Fidelity
December .	. Turquoise .	. Prosperity

The signs of the Zodiac also had a jewel allotted to each, the awards here being as follows :

Aries .	.	. Ruby
Taurus	.	. Topaz
Gemini	.	. Carbuncle
Cancer	.	. Emerald
Leo .	.	. Sapphire
Virgo .	.	. Diamond
Libra .	.	. Jacinth
Scorpio	.	. Agate
Sagittarius .		. Amethyst
Capricornus		. Beryl
Aquarius	.	. Onyx
Pisces .	.	. Jasper

So now, if you wish your husband, fiancé, or parent to buy you a precious stone, you know exactly which one to choose !

A—Zoo
No. 10. The Zebra

The Zebra's black-out stripes were there
Before the menace from the air.

Two by Two

HAVE you ever noticed how, at a dinner, or any other function where the ladies and gentlemen are placed alternately, sooner or later during the evening the men all manage to get together and the ladies somehow gravitate into a little group, too ?

Well, here's your chance to arrange a little grouping of the same type. Take four lumps of sugar and four nuts and arrange them alternately like this :

(Of course you can use ladies and gentlemen instead, if you like —and if you've got as many as that in the house !)

Now the problem is to re-arrange them so that all four lumps of sugar and all four nuts are together, but—and here's the difficulty—you must always move two neighbours together. If you're very clever, you'll find that you can take them two by two and accomplish the change-over in four moves.

" *Do you fly ?* "
" *No.*"
" *Cycle ?* "
" *No.*"
" *Drive a car ?* "
" *No, I don't do anything dang——*"
" *Sorry, sir ; since the black-out we don't insure pedestrians.*"

Kiddicorner

Advice to Those about to be rationed

DID you hear about the lady who wrote to one of her tradesman asking for advice on what to do when the commodity he sold was rationed ?

He sent her a reply on a post-card, and this is what it said :

If the Bmt put :
If the B. putting :

Can you guess who sent it and what he was trying to say ?

You can't black-out the Stars

No. 10. Libra

(the Balance, or Scales)

Between Virgo and Scorpio hang the four stars which make up the Scales.

The House of Lords

HAVE you ever wondered how it feels to address the House of Lords?

Disraeli knew.

When a young peer asked him what he could do to fit himself to address that august body, he replied:

" Have you a graveyard near your house? "

" Yes," said the peer.

" Then," continued Disraeli, " I recommend you to visit it early in the morning and practise on the tombstones."

Strictly Personal

No. 9. Adolf Hitler

When Adam delved and Eve span
Who was then the Aryan?

Hands across the Black-out

FAR from being an inconvenience, the black-out is of positive assistance in some games—particularly in one I fondly call " Hands across the Black-out." This can be played either by two teams, each selecting articles to puzzle the other, or by the entire gathering, with one person providing the test-pieces.

The room is plunged in darkness—that should be easy !—and the person in control begins to hand round a series of objects which the players have to identify entirely from their sense of touch. (Scent and taste are barred.)

If the articles are ingeniously selected, this can be a most uproarious game. Two suggestions :

A rubber glove filled with sand.

A sponge wrapped in a silk handkerchief.

THE MOUSE'S PETITION

OH ! hear a pensive prisoner's prayer
  For liberty that sighs ;
    And never let thine heart be shut
  Against the wretch's cries.

For here, forlorn and sad, I sit
  Within the wiry grate,
And tremble at the approaching morn
  Which brings impending fate.

If e'er thy breast with freedom glowed,
  And spurned a tyrant's chain,
Let not thy strong, oppressive force
  A free-born mouse detain !

Oh ! do not stain with guiltless blood
  Thy hospitable hearth !
Nor triumph that thy wiles betrayed
  A prize so little worth.

Thy scattered gleanings of a feast
  My frugal meals supply ;
But if thine unrelenting heart
  That slender boon deny—

The cheerful light, the vital air,
  Are blessings widely given ;
Let Nature's commoners enjoy
  The common gifts of heaven.

* * * *

So, when Destruction lurks unseen,
  Which men, like mice, may share,
May some kind angel clear thy path,
  And break the hidden snare.

A. L. BARBAULD

Dad's Telescope

JUST before Christmas Dad was in a London store, when he saw the *Black-out Book*, and decided to buy a copy.

On the next counter were some toy telescopes, and he decided that he'd have one of those, too. He asked the assistant to post the book and the telescope to him.

Dad noticed from the bill that the book and the postage together came to the same amount in pence and shillings as the telescope cost in shillings and pence. He paid with a pound note and the change came to exactly the same amount as the book and the postage, while the postage cost exactly nine shillings less than the telescope.

How much was each item?

———

The Letter E

The beginning of Eternity,
The end of Time and Space;
The beginning of every End
The end of every Race.

———

It is a truth well known to most,
That whatsoever thing is lost,
We search it e'er it come to light,
In every cranny but the right.
                              COWPER

———

Treason doth never prosper!
    What's the reason?
For, if it prosper—none dare call
    it treason.
            Sir JOHN HARRINGTON

A—Zoo

No. 11. The Lion

The Equator is an imaginary
Lion running round the earth.
                    SCHOOLBOY HOWLER

The Ubiquitous Matches!

Meet the ubiquitous matches.

Five in number, they make up an amazing combination of other numbers, if you arrange them correctly.

Here they make 141—but it might just as easily be 411, or 114, or even—by using Roman numerals—III.

Now see if you can make them produce, 4, 1, and 0.

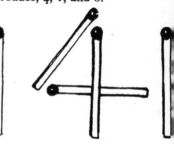

The Sky Signs have gone

THE black-out has spread its velvet blanket over the sky signs of Piccadilly Circus and a hundred other thoroughfares—and how we miss them ! Were they an eyesore, or things of beauty ? This is what G. K. Chesterton thought :

"As a matter of art for art's sake, they seem to me rather artistic. As a form of practical social work they seem to me stark, stupid waste. If Mr Bilge is rich enough to build a tower four hundred feet high and give it a crown of golden crescents and crimson stars, in order to draw attention to his manufacture of the Paradise Tooth Paste or the Seventh-heaven Cigar, I do not feel the least disposition to thank him for any serious form of social service. I have never tried the Seventh-heaven Cigar ; indeed, a premonition moves me towards the belief that I shall go down to the dust without trying it. I have every reason to doubt whether it does any particular good to those who smoke it, or any good to anybody except those who sell it. In short, Mr Bilge's usefulness consists in being useful to Mr Bilge, and the rest is illusion and sentimentalism."

There lives more faith in honest doubt,
Believe me, than in half the creeds.

TENNYSON

Infant Joy

I HAVE no name,
 I am but two days old."
What shall I call thee ?
 "I happy am,
 Joy is my name."
Sweet joy befall thee !

 Pretty Joy !
Sweet Joy, but two days old !
Sweet Joy I call thee.
 Thou dost smile,
 I sing the while,
Sweet joy befall thee !
 WILLIAM BLAKE

" Here's sixpence. Go and evacuate yourself."

Shunt that Train !

HAVE you ever wondered what would happen if two trains, going in opposite directions, met each other on a single-line track ?

Well, here it is ; happening right in front of your eyes ! Both trains are in a great hurry ; neither wants to go back to where the line is double. How can they get past each other ? The solution is obviously the little shunting-track, but that only holds six coaches, and both trains consist of an engine and six coaches.

There is a way of doing it, however ; and if you can spot it, you can arrange for Train A to pass Train B without very much difficulty.

The best way to work out this puzzle is to use half a dozen nuts or dominoes for the trucks and a reel of cotton of a different colour for each of the engines. Then you can move them about without any difficulty—and after one or two attempts you'll find your opinion of railway shunters rising rapidly !

Strictly Personal

No. 10. Greta Garbo

Leave her alone
And she'll come home,
Bringing her mail behind her.

EPITAPH

Warm summer sun, shine kindly here ;
Warm southern wind, blow softly here ;
Green sod above, lie light, lie light ;
Good-night, dear heart, good-night, good-night.

What's in a Name?

IS your Christian name one that fills you with embarrassment and disgust every time you write it?

Do you try your best to conceal it behind terse initials?

If so, the best thing for you to do is to arrange immediately to become Chinese. In China they have the pleasant and civilized custom of giving a child a ' milk ' name which it can discard when it grows to years of wisdom.

Think it over, Mr George Washington Smith, or Miss Victoria Mafeking Jones!

You can't black-out the Stars

No. 11. Capricornus (the He-Goat or Sea-Goat)

Capricornus lies between the Water-carrier and the Archer, and is best seen in the autumn.

DUST

THERE'S dust upon the mantel-shelf, the window-ledge, the stairs; flick it off the sideboard and you'll find it on the chairs. There's not a nook or cranny that it fails to settle in. No matter how you fight it, the dust will always win. Yet watch it floating lightly along a yellow beam! The sunshine seems to set it dancing in her golden stream, and what you thought an eyesore, to banish from your sight, has now become a thing of beauty, glittering and bright. The world is full of people we dislike as much as dust—we hardly like to speak to them unless we really must. They may cause us much annoyance and even some distress, but watch how different they become in the light of friendliness!

Blacking-out the Windows

A SHOPKEEPER, anxious to appear to comply with the black-out regulations, and at the same time anxious to show off his goods, decided to black-out half his window only. (This must have been before the police became really strict !)

He called in the local handyman, and said : " You see this window—it is five feet square. I want you to black-out half of it, but leave as much space as possible for showing off my goods."

The handyman looked at the window for a moment, and replied :

" I'll tell you what I can do. I'll black out half the window and still leave you a clear space five feet wide, five feet high and square."

The shopkeeper was naturally very pleased. How did the handyman do it ?

Measure It with Your Eye!

HERE'S a strange little optical illusion you may not have met before.

Measure these distances with your eye and you'll be positive that the space between B and C is much greater than the space between A and B, or C and D.

Now measure it with a ruler and notice the difference in the result.

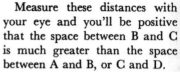
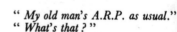

" My old man's A.R.P. as usual."
" What's that ? "
" 'Angin' Round Pubs."

A BIRTHDAY

MY heart is like a singing bird
  Whose nest is in a water'd shoot ;
My heart is like an apple-tree
  Whose boughs are bent with thick-set fruit ;
My heart is like a rainbow shell
  That paddles in a halcyon sea ;
My heart is gladder than all these,
  Because my love is come to me.

Raise me a dais of silk and down ;
  Hang it with vair and purple dyes ;
Carve it in doves and pomegranates,
  And peacocks with a hundred eyes ;
Work it in gold and silver grapes,
  In leaves and silver fleur-de-lys ;
Because the birthday of my life
  Is come, my love, is come to me.

CHRISTINA ROSSETTI

No More Birthdays

When any member of President Roosevelt's family attains the age of twenty-one he forthwith ceases to have any more birthdays—at least as far as public celebration of them is concerned. Birthday cakes and presents are thereafter forbidden.

A—Zoo

No. 12. The Kangaroo

The Kangaroo does sound a Bounder.

Strange Steps

THE little flight of steps at the bottom of this column may not be useful—you no sooner get to the top than you start coming down again—but it does provide an interesting problem.

By a simple operation you can cut up these steps into four pieces, all exactly equal in size and shape, which will fit together to form a perfect square.

If you don't want to damage or mark this book, place a piece of ordinary writing-paper over the drawing, and you will find that you can trace the outline through it quite easily and begin cutting to your heart's content !

'Tis with our judgments as our watches—none
Goes just alike—yet each believes his own.

POPE

Strictly Personal
No. 11. Godfrey Winn

Sunday morn,
Came the dawn—
Welcome in
Godfrey Winn !

Missing Statesmen

SEVEN statesmen and generals are missing—seven world-famous personalities—but you will find them all concealed in the strange jumble of meaningless words quoted below.

Hurry, now ! Because the world can't get along without at least five or six of them !

1. MILE NAG.
2. TROG.
3. I MALE BRANCH.
4. RICH HULLC.
5. HOB SHALE IRE.
6. NEED.
7. THE RIL.

Forgotten Money

YOU'D hardly believe it, but lots of people apparently go around this world depositing money in banks, and then forgetting all about it.

In the national banks of the United States alone the amount of unclaimed balances totals more than £20,000,000, in sums ranging from a few shillings to thousands of pounds.

Most of them are believed to have belonged to people who put aside a nest-egg and died before they could either use it or tell their relatives about it.

You can't black-out the Stars

No. 12. Aquarius
(the Water-carrier)

Aquarius, between Pisces and Capricornus, hangs high in the south-west in the autumn sky.

GIFTS

GIVE a man a horse he can ride,
  Give a man a boat he can sail,
And his rank and wealth, his strength and health,
  On sea nor shore shall fail.

Give a man a pipe he can smoke,
  Give a man a book he can read,
And his home is bright with a calm delight,
  Though the room be poor indeed.

Give a man a girl he can love,
  As I, O my love, love thee,
And his heart is great, with the pulse of Fate,
  At home, on land, on sea.

JAMES THOMSON

GENTLEMEN! I

The Royal Toast

The King, God bless him !

* * *

Toast to the Pretender

God bless the King, I mean the faith's defender ;
God bless—no harm in blessing—the Pretender ;
But who pretender is, or who is king—
God bless us all—that's quite another thing.

J. BYROM

* * *

Saxon Toast

This is ther custom and hev gest
When they are at the ale or fest :
Ilk man that levis gware him drink
Salle say " Wosseile " to him drink ;
He that biddis sall say "Wassaile,"
The tother salle say again " Drinkaille."
That says " Woisseile " drinks of the cup,
Kiss and his felaw he gives it up.

ROBERT DE BRUNNE

* * *

Ben Jonson's Toast

Drink to me only with thine eyes,
And I will pledge with mine ;
Or leave a kiss but in the cup,
And I'll not look for wine.

Shakespeare's Toast

Now, good digestion wait on appetite,
And health on both !

* * *

Sheridan's Toast

Here's to the maiden of bashful fifteen,
Here's to the widow of fifty ;
Here's to the flaunting, extravagant quean,
And here's to the housewife that's thrifty.
Let the toast pass ;
Drink to the lass ;
I'll warrant she'll prove an excuse for the glass.

TOAST

A name to which guests are invited to drink as a compliment. The word comes from the piece of toast which used at one time to be put into a cup of wine and which is still to be seen on ceremonial occasions. The toast originally was always a lady, who was credited with being the toast—or savour—of the wine.

GIVE YOU A TOAST!

Toast to Dickens

Though a pledge I had to shiver,
   And the longest ever was,
Ere his vessel leaves our river
   I would drink a health to Boz.

* * *

True Lover's Toast

   I have known many,
   Liked few,
   Loved one—
   Here's to you.

* * *

Old Scottish Toast

Here's to you, as good as you are,
And here's to me, as bad as I am,
But as good as you are and as
   bad as I am,
I'm as good as you are, as bad
   as I am.

BUMPER

A glass filled to the brim
with wine.

When the English were
good Catholics, they usually
drank the Pope's health in a
full glass every day after
dinner—*au bon père :* whence
Bumper.   Cocchi

When the glass is so full
that the wine bumps up in
the middle.

   Dr Arnold

Musical Toast

Here's a
health unto
his Majesty,
   With a fa-la-la-la-la, boys.
Confusion to his enemies,
   With a fa-la-la-la-la, boys.
And he who will not pledge the
   King
We wish for him no better thing
Than that he lack what now we
   sing,
   With a fa-la-la, etc.

* * *

Drunkard's Toast

Through the teeth and round
   the gums
Look out, tummy, here it comes !

* * *

Why and how Men drink

If on thy theme I rightly think,
There are five reasons why men
   drink :
Good wine, a friend, because I'm
   dry,
Or lest I should be by-and-by,
Or any other reasons why.
           H. Aldrich

I drink no more than a sponge.
           Rabelais

Correct Me if I'm Wrong

EVERYTHING there is to say has been said already, complain those young writers who have nothing to say in any case—but it is quite true that the speech of all of us is garnished with quotations from people who have said what we want to say and said it better than ever we could.

The trouble with quotations is that the misplacing of a single word may alter entirely what the original author intended to say. And if you traced many quotations back to the original source, you'd be surprised how differently they read.

Here are a dozen much-quoted passages, each given incorrectly. Can you spot the errors?

1. One touch of humour makes the whole world kin.

2. The quality of mercy is not strain'd ;
   It droppeth like the gentle dew from heaven.

3. How are the mighty fallen in the middle of the struggle !

4. Farewell, a last farewell, to all my grandeur !

5. The evil that men do lives after them,
   The good is oft-times buried in their graves !

6. Sleep, that knits up the ravell'd coat of care.

7. O sleep ! it is a lovely thing,
   Beloved from pole to pole.

8. Drink to me only with thine eyes,
   And I shall drink with mine.

9. Not a drum was heard, not a funeral note
   As his corpse to the ramparts we hurried.

10. Hell hath no fury like a woman scorned.

11. " Why that I do not know," said he ;
    " But 'twas a famous victory."

12. When Britons first, at heaven's command,
    Arose from out the azure main.

As a postscript to this little exercise, here are two lines you'll remember :

O woman ! in our hours of ease,
Uncertain, coy, and hard to please.

But do you know the two lines which follow them in Scott's poem ?

" *The Captain says you'd better read this before you decide whether you want to be rescued.*"

Kiddicorner

The Foursquare Pennies

THIS is a little trick you can try on your friends at school (when you have four pennies between you), or on visiting Uncles and Aunts. The latter are recommended, because they will occasionally provide the pennies for the trick and then decide that you are so clever that you had better keep them !

All you need is four ordinary British pennies. Spread these out on the table with the heads uppermost and ask your victim to make an exact square with them. When he has failed miserably, turn the pennies over and arrange them like this :

On the Collar of a Dog Pope gave to his Royal Highness

I am his Highness's dog at Kew,
Pray tell me, sir, whose dog are you ?

A—Zoo

No. 13. The Deer

That deer, dear, is a very dear deer,
But not so dear as that dear deer, dear.
Dear, dear, no !

The Boss

YOU think the boss has nothing to do ?

According to the general manager of an insurance company (Mr. J. Dyer Simpson) the boss's job consists merely of :

Deciding what is to be done.

Telling somebody to do it.

Listening to the reasons why it should not be done, or should be done differently, or by someone else.

Following up to see if it· has been done.

Inquiring why not.

Following up again.

Finding it done, but incorrectly.

Deciding that since it has been done, it may as well be left as it is.

Considering how much simpler and better it would have been to do it himself in the first place.

You can't black-out the Stars

No. 13. Leo (the Lion)

On the other side of the Virgin from the Serpent hangs Leo. Part of Leo is sometimes known as the Sickle—four of the stars roughly forming the outline—while Regulus is the brightest of the constellation.

Pope foresees the Black-out

Nor public flame, nor private, dares to shine,
Nor human light is left, nor glimpse divine !
Lo ! thy dread Empire, Chaos, is restored :
Light dies before thine uncreating word :
Thy hand, great Anarch, lets the curtain fall ;
And universal darkness buries all.
Dunciad

Strictly Personal

No. 12. Anna Neagle

The Queen, God bless her ! stands among her peers—
How young she looks for Sixty Glorious Years !

Kiddicorner

The Eternal Triangle

NOW then, youngsters ! Have you heard your Mother or Father speak of the Eternal Triangle ? Well, here it is !

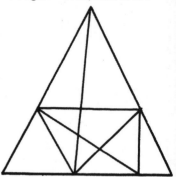

What you have to do is to find out how many triangles there are altogether in the drawing. And don't say " eight," because it's many more than that !

THE OLD FAMILIAR FACES

I HAVE had playmates, I have had companions,
In my days of childhood, in my joyful schooldays—
All, all are gone, the old familiar faces.

I have been laughing, I have been carousing,
Drinking late, sitting late, with my bosom cronies—
All, all are gone, the old familiar faces.

I loved a Love once, fairest among women :
Closed are her doors on me, I must not see her—
All, all are gone, the old familiar faces.

I have a friend, a kinder friend has no man :
Like an ingrate, I left my friend abruptly ;
Left him, to muse on the old familiar faces.

Ghost-like I paced round the haunts of my childhood,
Earth seem'd a desert I was bound to traverse,
Seeking to find the old familiar faces.

Friend of my bosom, thou more than a brother,
Why wert not thou born in my father's dwelling ?
So might we talk of the old familiar faces—

How some they have died, and some they have left me,
And some are taken from me ; all are departed—
All, all are gone, the old familiar faces.

CHARLES LAMB

Can You draw a Square?

CAN you draw a square, or an easy design like the one on this page?

Of course you can—anyone can—but try doing it this way!

Take a pencil and paper and a mirror. Now, holding the mirror in your left hand, try to draw the square with your right, but—and here's the rub—you must look only in the mirror at the reflection of what you are drawing.

Here is the way to do it, illustrated by Woods—

Woods wasted a whole afternoon trying to do it, so don't be surprised if it takes you a little while to master it.

The Things They say

Experience is not what happens to a man. It is what a man does with what happens to him.

ALDOUS HUXLEY

* * *

There are two things to aim at in life : first, to get what you want ; and after that, to enjoy it. Only the wisest achieve the second.

LOGAN PEARSALL SMITH

* * *

Everything I know about her is merely daresay.

ALEXANDER WOOLLCOTT

* * *

Mother, my foot feels just like gassy lemonade.

ANY FIVE-YEAR-OLD

* * *

The parent who could see his boy as he really is would shake his head and say : " Willie is no good ; I'll sell him."

STEPHEN LEACOCK

A—Zoo

No. 14. The Rabbit

*All well-bred Rabbits
Sport riding habits.*

The Happy Man

Happy the man, and happy he
    alone,
He who can call to-day his own ;
He who, secure within, can say,
To-morrow do thy worst, for I
    have lived to-day.

DRYDEN

---

*" You're back very quickly—did
you carry out instructions ? "*

*" Yes, sir ; I flew over Berlin and
dropped those parcels of leaflets over
the side."*

*" What ! You dropped them still
done up in the parcels ? "*

" Yes, sir."

*" But, good Lord, man ! You
might have killed somebody ! "*

I'll pay You Back

HERE'S a knotty little money
problem for you.

Supposing you lent a man £20
(that is always supposing you had
£20 to lend him), and he said :
" Look here, old chap, I'll pay
you back half of the money next
week and half of the balance
outstanding every week after that
—that's £10 next week, £5 the
week after, £2 10s. the week
after that, and so on."

Would you accept the offer ?

And how long would it take
him to pay off the full £20 ?

Man is not the creature of
circumstances : circumstances are
the creatures of men.

DISRAELI

Picture of Events

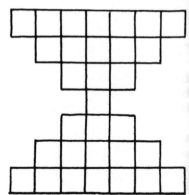

HERE'S a simple problem for those of you who read your daily papers.

All you are required to do is to fill each of the lines of squares on the accompanying diagram with a word of the requisite length. If you do so correctly, the middle letters of each word, with the addition of one letter in the middle square, will confirm that you have a clear picture of events in your mind.

Reading from top to bottom, the required war-words are: 1. A famous British naval town; 2. The German economic adviser; 3. A brilliant airman; 4. A Polish river; 5. A sea in which naval battles have been fought. 6. An Allied commander.

* * *

Achievement

Between the idea
And the reality,
Between the motion
And the act
Falls the shadow.

T. S. ELIOT

* * *

My real judgment of my own work is that I have spoilt a number of jolly good ideas in my time.

G. K. CHESTERTON

* * *

Strictly Personal

No. 13. Basil Dean

I adore Basil Dean—
Though he doesn't get younger—
But much more than Basil
I love his son Gunga.

Chess-board Solo

THIS is a game which anyone can play alone, with a chess-board—or, if there is no board at hand, with a piece of paper ruled into 64 squares (eight by eight).

All you are required to do is to take eight pawns (eight draughts-men, or counters, or lumps of sugar will do equally well) and place them on the board so that none of them is in the same line as any of the others, either horizontally, vertically, or diagonally. There are several solutions, but none of them is easy to find.

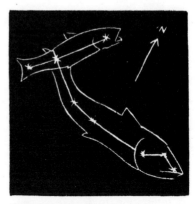

You can't black-out the Stars

No. 14. Pisces (the Fishes)

The Fishes you will find between Aquarius and Aries.

'Tis all a Chequer-board

'TIS all a Chequer-board of Nights and Days
Where Destiny with Men for Pieces plays :
Hither and thither moves, and mates, and slays,
And one by one back in the Closet lays.

The Ball no Question makes of Ayes and Noes,
But Right or Left as strikes the Player goes ;
And He that toss'd Thee down into the Field,
He knows about it all—He knows—He knows !

EDWARD FITZGERALD

Is Your Name Jack?

NOBODY seems to know just why, but our forefathers always used the names Jack and Tom slightingly. If there was any mischief afoot, Jack was blamed. If anyone was dull or backward, he was called Tom.

Just at the moment we are concerned only with Jack, and it is interesting to look back into history and find Jack-in-office, Jack Adams, Jack-a-dreams, Jack-of-all-trades (and master of none), as reminders of this peculiar prejudice.

Actually, of course, Jack is a ubiquitous person to be found in scores of interesting situations—and that provides us with a little brains-test this evening. Can you find a word consisting of Jack and a few additional letters to supply the correct answer to each of the following definitions? Remember, each answer must contain the word JACK, spelt correctly and with the letters in their right order.

1. An ordinary seaman.
2. A bird like a crow.
3. A garment worn by men.
4. A masculine donkey.
5. A broad pancake.
6. A carnivorous animal.
7. A German officer's footwear.
8. A Boy Scout's most-prized possession.
9. A travelling Woolworth store.
10. An impertinent young person.

One last word to those whose name is Jack. There is an old proverb that says : " A good Jack makes a good Jill," and it's no good your saying you have no Jill, for Shakespeare has already told us that " every Jack shall have his Jill " !

A—Zoo

No. 15. The Moose

And the mountain brought forth a Moose.

SCOTTISH PROVERB

Pronunciation is Vexation

THE words most often mis-pronounced by the average person, say experts, include—

Data, Gratis, Gondola, Impious, Chic, Halcyon.

You think you know them all perfectly? Then check your pronunciation with the dictionary. You may be in for a surprise.

But don't worry if you're wrong. Only eight or nine people in every million get them correct every time—and even the B.B.C. Committee of Experts can't agree on the right pronunciation of some quite ordinary words.

" Look, John! We're getting near civilization! "

Of all the types in the world, the worst is the sort that goes about telling you truths for your good.

HUGH WALPOLE

VISITORS

EVERY morning in the garden I have guests to entertain.
They're really uninvited, but don't think that I complain
—for breadcrumbs are delicious to a sparrow, I suppose, and
tasty bits of bacon fat are tempting, goodness knows! It's
pleasant playing hostess to my feathered friends this way—
" It's only cupboard love," I can hear some people say—
but to me the scraps I give them seem a poor recompense
for their cheerful little voices in this world of dissonance.

FAMILIAR

The Hare and the Hound

A Hound having put up a Hare from a bush, chased her for some distance, but the Hare had the best of it, and got off. A Goatherd who was passing jeered at the Hound, saying that the Hare was the better runner of the two. " You forget," replied the Hound, " that it is one thing to be running for your dinner, and another to be running for your life."

* * *

The Wolf and the Sheep

A Wolf that had been bitten by a dog, and was in a very sad case, being unable to move, called to a Sheep, who was passing by, and begged her to fetch him some water from a neighbouring stream. " For if you," said he, " will only bring me drink, I will find meat for myself." " Yes," said the Sheep, " I make no doubt of it ; for, if I come near enough to give you the drink, you will soon make mincemeat of *me*."

The Dolphins and the Sprat

The Dolphins and the Whales were at war with one another. While the battle was at its height, the Sprat stepped in and endeavoured to separate them. But one of the Dolphins cried out, " Let us alone, friend ! We had rather perish in the contest than be reconciled by you ! "

* * *

The Lioness

The Beasts were disputing which could boast of the largest family. Presently they came to the Lioness. " And how many," said they, " do you have at a birth ? " " One," said she, grimly, " but that one is a Lion."

Quality comes before Quantity.

* * *

The Falconer and the Partridge

A Falconer having taken a Partridge in his net, the bird cried out sorrowfully, " Let me go, good Master Falconer, and I promise you I will decoy other Partridges into your net." " No," said the man, " whatever I might have done, I am now determined not to spare you ; for there is no death too bad for him who is ready to betray his friends."

FABLES

The Arab and the Camel

An Arab, having loaded his Camel, asked him whether he preferred to go up hill or down hill. " Pray, Master," said the Camel, " is the straight way across the plain shut up ? "

* * *

The Mole and her Mother

Said a young Mole to her mother, " Mother, I can see." So, in order to try her, her mother put a lump of frankincense before her, and asked her what it was. " A stone," said the young one. " Oh, my child ! " said the Mother, " not only do you not see, but you cannot even smell."

Brag about one defect, and betray another.

* * *

The Moon and her Mother

The Moon once asked her mother to make her a little cloak that would fit her well. " How," replied she, " can I make you a cloak to fit you, who are now a New Moon, and then a Full Moon, and then again neither one nor the other ? "

The Dog in the Manger

A Dog made his bed in a Manger, and lay snarling and growling to keep the horses from their provender. " See," said one of them, " what a miserable cur it is who neither can eat corn himself, nor will allow those to eat it who can."

* * *

The Gnat and the Bull

A Gnat that had been buzzing about the head of a Bull, and had at length settled himself down upon the Bull's horn, begged his pardon for incommoding him. " If," says he, " my weight at all inconveniences you, pray say so, and I will be off in a moment." " Oh, never trouble your head about that," says the Bull, " for 'tis all one to me whether you go or stay ; and, to say the truth, I did not know you were there."

The smaller the Mind the greater the Conceit.

We'll go no More a-roving

SO, we'll go no more a-roving
  So late into the night,
Though the heart be still as loving,
  And the moon be still as bright.

For the sword outwears its sheath,
  And the soul wears out the breast,
And the heart must pause to breathe,
  And love itself have rest.

Though the night were made for loving,
  And the day returns too soon,
Yet we'll go no more a-roving
  By the light of the moon.

LORD BYRON

What's Wrong with your Eyes?

WHY, whatever's wrong with my eyes?" cried Mother, as she looked at the drawing below. " I can see grey shadows at the corners of the squares ! "

Take a look for yourself. Can you see grey shadows there, too ?

Then what's wrong with your eyes ?

The answer is " Nothing," of course. It's a simple optical illusion caused by the violent contrast of the black and white and the narrow space between the black squares.

Truth may often be stranger than fiction, but it is seldom as artistic.

CHARLES LOW

Come to another Full Stop

HERE is a second unpunctuated passage for you to try on the family one by one. All they have to do is to put in the correct punctuation as they read it aloud.

Wooderson made a new record for the mile with his feet on the mantelpiece a bachelor feels really at home in a girls school the mistresses have full charge of their pupils and teach them gambling drunkenness and other misdemeanours are punished by law by laws are made by local councils to suit local conditions such as could spare the time attended the film show given for the blind the concert was a great success until the revolution russia was governed by the tzar.

Strictly Personal
No. 14. Paul Muni

Actors great and actors puny
Have to hand the palm to Muni.

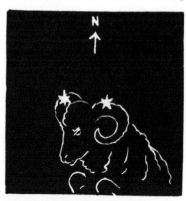

You can't black-out the Stars
No. 15. Aries (the Ram)

Aries got its name from the Latin word for battering-ram (which had a ram's head carved on the end of it). The constellation lies between Taurus and Pisces—the Bull and the Fishes.

So now you know

EVERY ONE wants to understand art. Why not try to understand the song of a bird ? Why does one love the night, flowers, everything around one, without trying to understand them ? Whereas with painting, people must *understand*. If only they would realize above all that an artist works of necessity ; that he himself is only a trifling bit of the world, and that no more importance should be attributed to him than to plenty of other things that please us in the world, though we cannot explain them.

PICASSO

What's in a Name?

And last of all an admiral came,
A terrible man, with a terrible name ;
A name which you all know by sight very well,
But which no one can speak and no one can spell.

SOUTHEY

THE great disadvantage of fame is the shortness of the human memory—ask any film star !

How many of us can say exactly who was the last Prime Minister but one ? How many remember the name of the man who wrote last year's best-seller, or appeared in that film we liked so much in 1929, or flew the Atlantic in 1934 ?

You think you can ? Then try yourself out on these questions. All I ask for is thirteen well-known names.

1. Who was the Swan of Avon ?
2. Who was the G.O.M. ?
3. Who was the Iron Duke ?
4. Which statesman was dizzy ?
5. Which two twentieth-century notabilities have been known as ' the Tiger ' ?
6. Who gave his name to a travelling-case ?
7. Which horse-drawn carriage was christened after which queen ?
8. Which European statesman is best remembered as a herring ?
9. Which President gave his name to a motor-car ?
10. Which famous Catholic dignitary is remembered as underwear ?
11. Can you name another European statesman whose name is associated with a certain form of steak ?
12. Which prince gave his name to a watch-chain ?

A—Zoo

No. 16. The Antelope

You could never kid an antelope
By calling a melon a cantaloupe.

Don't waste Matches !

HERE'S one of the simplest match tricks we've had so far.

Take ten matches and arrange them like this to make five.

Now can you take the same ten matches and arrange them to make four ?

" Our one desire is for peace."
" Yes, I know—a piece for you and a piece for him."

OF GARDENS

AND because the breath of Flowers is far sweeter in the air (where it comes and goes like the warbling of Musick) than in the hand, therefore nothing is more fit for that delight than to know what be the flowers and plants that do best perfume the air. Roses, damask and red, are fast flowers of their smells ; so that you may walk by a whole row of them, and find nothing of their sweetness ; yea, though it be in a morning's dew. Bays likewise yield no smell as they grow, Rosemary little, nor Sweet Marjoram ; that which above all others yields the sweetest smell in the air is the Violet, especially the White Double Violet, which comes twice a year, about the middle of *April* and about *Bartholomew-tide.*   FRANCIS BACON

BALLOONS

I REACHED the summit of the hill and paused for well-earned rest. Beneath me lay the city by the noon-day sun caressed. I turned away and idly gazed upon the cloudless sky, then caught my breath in wonderment, for up there, riding high, balloons in countless numbers hung serenely, row on row. They shone like burnished silver as I watched them from below; but later, when the sun went down, they caught each burning ray and flushed from grey to crimson—then back again to grey. They gave the clear impression of being really free, yet they were tethered to the earth by cords, invisibly. The wise men and philosophers are like them, I have found, for though their heads are in the clouds, their feet are on the ground.

Kiddicorner

The Answer's a —?

THIS is another little trick you can try on your friends — and enemies, if you have any.

Ask them to tell you any word which looks exactly the same whether it is looked at in the normal way, or upside down.

After several attempts, they'll tell you there is no such word. You then assure them that there is—and that it is a perfect description of them. Here it is:

chump

(Of course, you must be careful to write it with a single stroke for 'H' and to see that the 'C' and the second half of the 'P' are exactly the same size. A little practice will soon ensure this.)

Improve your Figure !

THIS is one of those mathematical oddities which has been used ever since mankind began to count, as a means of mystifying every one who has not already heard of it for himself.

Ask your intended victim to write down the figures one to nine in that order. Now get him to say which of the figures he considers least well executed. Assuming that he chooses 3, get him to multiply the whole row by 3 and the resultant answer by 9.

If he chooses any other number, he must multiply first by that and then by 9. Whichever he chooses, the answer will be the same—a useful exercise in improving his figure !

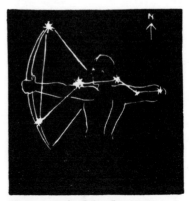

You can't black-out the Stars

No. 16. Sagittarius (the Archer)

Named after the light-arm infantry of the Roman army, Sagittarius hangs between Scorpio and Capricornus. It is seen at its best in the summer.

The Things They say

An Englishman in a soft shirt will think like blazes ; the mere putting on of a stiff one indicates to him that he has finished for the day.   JAMES AGATE

* * *

Be wiser than other people if you can, but do not tell them so.
  LORD CHESTERFIELD

* * *

Wisdom is knowing what to do next ; Skill is knowing how to do it ; and Virtue is doing it.
  D. S. JORDAN

* * *

Doughnuts are a deep, natural desire of the human race.
  SAMUEL J. LEVITT

Strictly Personal

No. 15. Stalin

Said the Eagle to the Stalin :
 " Birds in their little nests agree."
Said the Stalin : " Yes, my darlin',
 So long as you agree with me ! "

A—Zoo

No. 16. The Crocodile
" Let me weep awhile,"
Said the Crocodile.

Debits and Credits

THE possession of a modest (but not large) income of her own is an aid to the ambition, independence, usefulness, and contentment of a woman and not a hindrance to her happy marriage. Whereas to a young man a small inheritance lessens ambition and self-reliance and often furnishes an excuse to spare himself the strenuous efforts and exertions without which a man cannot discover such talent as he has, or escape deterioration of character, or achieve any object in life worth attaining. Hardships, poverty, and want are the best incentives and the best foundation for the success of a man.

BRADFORD MERRILL

" *Do you want some petrol ?* "
" *Rather !* "
" *Okay—give us your lighter.*"

More Pluralities

WHEN a number of bishops, or jurymen, or ships, or books get together, there's a name for it.

How many of them do you know ?

Here's a list of fourteen for you to try your hand on :

1. A —— of bishops.
2. A —— of ships.
3. A —— of whales.
4. A —— of trees.
5. A —— of bushes.
6. A —— of people at church.
7. A —— of sailors.
8. A —— of rooms.
9. A —— of directors.
10. A —— of magistrates.
11. A —— of fish.
12. A —— of books.
13. A —— of goats.
14. A —— of jurymen.

Kiddicorner

The Three Wise Men

ONCE upon a time there were three wise men, but like most wise men they were touchy about little things, and one day they quarrelled about which of them was the tallest.

The quarrel was so bitter that they refused to walk along the street together, but walked a few steps ahead of one another, like this :

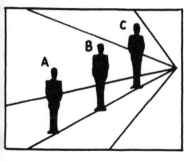

Can you settle the quarrel for them and decide who is really the tallest ?

If not, take a tape-measure, or ruler, and settle it once and for all.

Experience

The only thing Experience teaches us is that Experience teaches us nothing.

ANDRÉ MAUROIS

6

The Miller's Daughter

IT is the miller's daughter,
    And she is grown so dear,
        so dear,
That I would be the jewel
    That trembles in her ear :
For, hid in ringlets day and
        night,
I'd touch her neck so warm
        and white.

And I would be the girdle
    About her dainty dainty
        waist,
And her heart would beat
        against me,
    In sorrow and in rest :
And I should know if it beat
        right,
I'd clasp it round so close and
        tight.

And I would be the necklace,
    And all day long to fall and
        rise
Upon her balmy bosom,
    With her laughter or her sighs :
And I would lie so light, so light,
I scarce should be unclasp'd at
        night.

TENNYSON

What happened to the Shilling?

THIS is one of the neatest little problems I have heard for a long time.

It concerns three girls of the W.A.T.S.—or they can be V.A.D.s or W.R.N.S. if you prefer it—who decide to stay at an hotel one night during the black-out, because they have missed the last train back to their headquarters.

At the hotel they find that there is only one room vacant, but as this has two double beds in it, they decide to take it. The landlord charges them five shillings each for the night, and they go upstairs to bed.

After they have gone, the landlord reflects that he usually charges only ten shillings a night for that particular room and that it is probably unfair of him to charge the girls so much. So he calls the lift-boy, gives him five shillings, and tells him to take it up to the ladies, and explain that the room will only cost them a total of ten shillings.

On the way up to the room, the lift boy reflects that the girls will be quite satisfied with the return of a shilling each, and decides to pocket two shillings for himself, silencing his conscience with the thought that three into five won't go, in any case.

Arrived at the girls' room, he knocks on the door and hands them back one shilling each. They go to sleep quite happily, and the lift-boy spends his next afternoon off at the pictures with the stolen money.

But here's the point. The girls have now paid four shillings each (five shillings, less the one the lift-boy returned to them). Three times four shillings is twelve shillings. Right? And the lift-boy has two shillings, which makes a total of fourteen? Right? But originally they paid fifteen shillings, didn't they? Then what, in the name of goodness, happened to the other shilling?

Strictly Personal

No. 16. Ivor Brown

*Every play that comes to town
In the " Observer " is done Brown.*

Odd Jobs

No. 1. Ghost Manufacturers

Nearly a quarter of a million people in China are kept busy all the year round making paper ' ghosts ' for various Chinese religious ceremonials.

The ghosts may be in the form of furniture, or other possessions. These are burned, after various rituals, by the priest, and are then presumed to have arrived in the hereafter for the use of deceased friends or relatives of the purchasers.

———

Teach me the art of forgetting, for I often remember what I would not and cannot forget what I would.

THEMISTOCLES

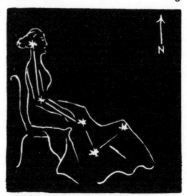

You can't black-out the Stars

No. 17. Cassiopeia
(the Seated Lady)

This constellation was named after the wife of Cepheus, king of Ethiopia, mother of Andromeda.

THE PLAIN MAN'S PRAYER

GIVE me a good digestion, Lord,
And also something to digest.
Give me a healthy body, Lord,
With sense to keep it at its best.

Give me a healthy mind, Lord,
To keep the good and pure in sight,
Which, seeing sin, is not appalled,
But finds a way to set it right.

Give me a mind that is not bored,
That does not whimper, whine, or sigh ;
Don't let me worry overmuch
About the fussy thing called I.

Give me a sense of humour, Lord ;
Give me the grace to see a joke.
To get some happiness from life
And pass it on to other folk.

Left by an unknown worshipper in Chester Cathedral

Let's go to Sleep

Sleep that knits up the ravell'd sleave of care.
                                    WILLIAM SHAKESPEARE

O bed! bed! delicious bed!
Thou heaven on earth to the weary head!
                                    THOMAS HOOD

S. T. Coleridge

O sleep! it is a gentle thing,
  Beloved from pole to pole!
To Mary, Queen, the praise be
      given!
She sent the gentle sleep from
      Heaven
  That slid into my soul.

John Fletcher

Come, Sleep, and with thy sweet
      deceiving
  Lock me in delight awhile;
  Let some pleasing dreams be-
      guile
  All my fancies; that from
      thence
I may feel an influence,
All my powers of care bereaving!

Thomas Dekker

Art thou poor, yet hast thou
      golden slumbers?
  O sweet content!
Art thou rich, yet is thy mind
      perplexed?
  O punishment!
Dost thou laugh to see how fools
      are vex'd
To add to golden numbers golden
      numbers?
  O sweet content! O sweet, O
      sweet content!

Sir Philip Sidney

Come, Sleep; O Sleep! the
      certain knot of peace.
  The baiting-place of wit, the
      balm of woe,
The poor man's wealth, the
      prisoner's release,
  Th' indifferent judge between
      the high and low;
With shield of proof shield me
      from out the prease
  Of those fierce darts Despair
      at me doth throw:
O make in me those civil wars
      to cease;
  I will good tribute pay, if thou
      do so.
Take thou of me smooth pillows,
      sweetest bed,
  A chamber deaf to noise and
      blind of light,
A rosy garland and a weary head;
  And if these things, as being
      thine by right,
    Move not thy heavy grace,
      thou shalt in me,
    Livelier   than   elsewhere,
      Stella's image see.

Cervantes

  Now blessings light on him that
first invented sleep! It covers a
man all over, thoughts and all,
like a cloak; it is meat for the
hungry, drink for the thirsty, heat
for the cold, and cold for the hot.

When Sleep won't come

WHAT do you do when sleep won't come?

Count sheep? So, says Gracie Allen, the comedienne, did she, but they " made such a noise baa-ing at me all night that I gave it up in despair. Now I count oranges on an imaginary orange tree, instead."

In *The Lives of a Bengal Lancer*, Yeats-Brown advises anyone suffering from insomnia to draw twenty even breaths and then hold the twenty-first breath as long as possible. Do this three or four times, he says, and you will be drowsy.

Lying in an absolutely relaxed position, with every muscle free from tension; then 'emptying' the mind and quietly reciting a well-known passage of prose, such as the Lord's Prayer, is another piece of advice for the sleepless. As an alternative to this you can try Lilian Gish's suggestion—black eyeshades and wax ear-plugs!

Reading the dullest book you can find is said to help. So is getting up and going for a quick walk — but how inconvenient!

Most unappetizing suggestion of all, by Katherine Mayo, the novelist, quoted in the *Reader's Digest*, is " Put about a half-teaspoonful of pepper in a coffee cup and fill the cup with blistering hot milk. You drink the milk immediately and as fast as you possibly can."

Good-night! Sleep well!

TO SLEEP

O SOFT embalmer of the still midnight,
    Shutting, with careful fingers and benign,
Our gloom-pleas'd eyes, embower'd from the light,
    Enshaded in forgetfulness divine :
O soothest Sleep, if so it pleases thee, close
    In midst of this thine hymn my willing eyes,
Or wait the " Amen," ere thy poppy throws
    Around my bed its lulling charities.
Then save me, or the passèd day will shine
Upon my pillow, breeding many woes,
    Save me from curious Conscience, that still lords
Its strength for darkness, burrowing like a mole ;
    Turn the key deftly in the oiled wards,
And seal the hushed Casket of my Soul.

                JOHN KEATS

ANSWER "YES" or "NO"

HERE are fifteen definite statements. How many are correct—yes or no?

1. It is fattening to drink milk.

2. Genius is akin to insanity.

3. Receipts need not be kept six years after the date of the payment.

4. The human brain goes on living for ten minutes after its owner's death.

5. The longest rôle in Shakespeare's plays is Richard II.

6. *Gunga Din* was a novel before it was a film.

7. The Chinese are the most numerous race on earth.

8. Every human being has more than 1000 direct ancestors.

9. Germany has more inhabitants to the square mile than Great Britain.

10. An ant can lift ten times its own weight.

11. A grasshopper can jump fifty times its own height.

12. Water boils at a lower temperature on the top of high mountains.

13. The present Duke of Windsor was once crowned King of England.

14. For any ordinary conversation, a total vocabulary of 850 words is sufficient.

15. A pound of gold weighs less than a pound of lead.

" *You're four hours late! Where have you been?* "

" *Well, sir, it was so quiet I went down and pushed a few leaflets under the doors!* "

So They say

A FAMOUS Swedish chemist is supposed to vouch for this story.

A peasant, about forty years of age, was found buried under snow. His clothing seemed to belong to a remote period. As the body was uninjured, prompt methods were employed to thaw it out and make its limbs flexible before dissection. To this end it was placed in a lecture-room, which had been warmed to a gentle heat, and was gently rubbed with alcohol. To the amazement of the onlookers it opened its eyes, sighed, breathed, and sat upright. In the end it was completely restored to life.

The man who had been so strangely revived reckoned that he had been lying for sixty-seven years under snow, in a deep ravine into which he had been hurled by a violent squall. He lived for another twenty years and made long journeys on foot, earning his living by telling the story of his ' death.'

A—Zoo
No. 18. The Elephant

*The Elephant never forgets, they say—
But this one forgot his trunk one day.*

Kiddicorner
Picture Puzzle

Can you guess what word this picture represents ?

Good taste is not instinctive, but acquired. All native tastes are bad. The taste of the young in music is abominable, in literature execrable. Good taste grows slowly through the effort to understand what is beyond us, the endeavour to appreciate what we cannot yet understand.

C. E. M. JOAD

EVACUEES

DAINTY little maiden, whither would you wander?
Whither from this pretty home, the home where mother dwells?
" Far and far away," said the dainty little maiden,
" All among the gardens, auriculas, anemones,
Roses and lilies and Canterbury-bells."
Dainty little maiden, whither would you wander?
Whither from this pretty house, this city-house of ours?
" Far and far away," said the dainty little maiden,
" All among the meadows, the clover and the clematis,
Daisies and kingcups and honeysuckle-flowers."

TENNYSON, *The City Child*

Strictly Personal
No. 17. The Crazy Gang
All that's Naughton is not Gold,
Twice times Flanagan's much too old,
Nervo takes some awful Knox
And Chesney Allen wears silk socks.
But who is which, we're rather hazy,
We only know the whole gang's crazy.

It sounds Easy!

YOU'VE heard of people whose hands are so strong that they can tear telephone directories in half? Well, here's a little trick that's much easier than that—but you'll be very clever if you can do it.

Take a sheet of newspaper and fold it eight times.

That's all!

And there's only one condition. Each fold must be completely across the paper (*i.e.* it must halve the remaining surface).

You can't black-out the Stars

No. 18. Corona Borealis
(the Northern Crown)

This constellation hangs midway between Hercules and Bootes.

Don't waste Matches !

Here are seventeen matches arranged to make eight squares.

Can you take away six matches and leave only two squares ?

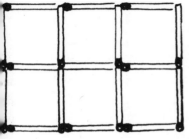

Chestnut Corner

HAVE you noticed how the oldest stories—and particularly the oldest jokes—are quite new to many of our friends ? Has it occurred to you, too, that every fifteen or twenty years a new generation is growing up, totally unaware—until we tell them—of those two thousand stories, moral and otherwise, which are stored away in our brains ? Can you think of a better opportunity for beginning the good work than these long black-out evenings ? And so the *Black-out Book* presents, with due acknowledgment to *Band Waggon*, its own cherished Chestnut Corner :

No. 1. Mark Twain signs the Register

One day when he arrived at a Canadian hotel, Mark Twain found that the person arriving before him had signed the register " Baron Blank and Valet."

He thought for a moment and then wrote : " Mark Twain and valise."

A—Zoo

No. 19. Panther

I know a lisping Panther
Who thinks Anton Dolin's a danther.

Odd Jobs

No. 2. Canning Rattlers

OUT in Florida, twelve men spend their entire working days catching rattlesnakes for the local canning factory, which sends out 10,000 tins of snake meat every year. The skins are also used for manufacturing handbags and other articles.

The use of rattlesnakes for food was discovered by chance, when a local farmer decided to skin and cook a rattler caught by his sons.

RETURN
of the Horse

THE other day I walked along a city thoroughfare and all at once I noticed it was looking strangely bare. The constant stream of cars had ceased, the hooting taxis gone. The winking traffic lights went off and presently went on. They seemed a little out of place—and then I heard the sound of heavy hoofs and creaking wheels behind me on the ground. I turned to find a horse and cart drawn up not far away. The mare was old and shaggy, with a faded coat of grey. Her eyes, benevolent and mild, drew mine instinctively. Where was that knob of sugar I was saving for my tea? I delved into my pocket and discovered it was there, then I handed it politely to that old grey mare. " I'm glad to see you back again upon the road once more, for you bring a moment's respite from the city's rush and roar ! "

Kiddicorner

Pass it on!

THIS game is a little more boisterous than most of those in this book, but great fun if you can persuade the whole family to play it just before bedtime.

All you need is the outer covers of two matchboxes. The party is then divided into two teams, the game being to pass the matchbox from nose to nose, as illustrated in the drawing, along the entire team more quickly than one's opponents. If the box is dropped or touched by hand, it must be returned to the beginning of the line again.

Another variation of this game is played with the players seated on two rows of chairs. The first players on either side have an orange which they balance between their ankles and endeavour to pass on to the next player without dropping it. This is recommended for strengthening the leg muscles.

The Things They say

Art, like morality, consists in drawing the line somewhere.

G. K. CHESTERTON

* * *

Aryan : a man born within the sound of Goeb-bells.

WILLIAM HICKEY

* * *

The whole art of life consists in knowing when to abandon with a good grace something that will one day be taken from you by force.

J. B. MORTON

* * *

Most people are akin to the old theologian who said that he was entirely open to conviction, but would like to see anyone who could convince him.

ERNEST R. TRATTNER

" *Says 'e always wanted to be a fireman, sir.*"

ADD-A-WORD

ONE of the easiest of round games — and one of the most provoking—is Add-a-Word.

Any number of players may take part, and no pencils, papers, or other properties are required.

The first player begins the game by speaking one word ; the second continues it by adding a second word ; each additional player provides one more, and the game goes on until such time as it is no longer possible for the next person to add a word which makes a grammatical continuation to those which have gone before.

The defaulting player may then concede one forfeit, or alternatively challenge the person who passed on the sentence to him to add a word. If that person is unable to do so, he pays the forfeit instead. If, however, he succeeds in doing so, the challenger pays two forfeits.

Here is an example from actual play :

" I met a man who was unable to read a book because he suffered from astigmatism, caused by neglect in early youth, and only partially overcome by treatment given by the most accomplished specialist in Europe at the time.'

In this particular game one player failed at the word ' Europe and challenged the player who handed him the word. That player hit upon the additional phrase ' at the time,' thus robbing the challenger of two forfeits.

I expect you all know the similar game in which a sentence is whispered from person to person round a room. If strict secrecy is observed, the wording of the message by the time it returns to the sender is a splendid little parable on the folly of believing word-of-mouth rumours !

Strictly Personal

No. 18. John Gielgud

You must never pronounce Gielgud
As though it referred to mud.
Be it always understood
It's nothing if not good.

MY BONNIE MARY

GO fetch to me a pint o' wine,
　An' fill it in a silver tassie,
That I may drink, before I go,
　A service to my bonnie lassie;
The boat rocks at the pier o' Leith;
　Fu' loud the wind blaws frae the ferry;
The ship rides by the Berwick-law,
　And I maun leave my bonnie Mary.

The trumpets sound, the banners fly,
　The glittering spears are rankèd ready;
The shouts o' war are heard afar,
　The battle closes thick and bloody;
But it's no the roar o' sea or shore
　Wad mak' me langer wish to tarry;
Nor shout o' war that's heard afar—
　It's leaving thee, my bonnie Mary!

ROBERT BURNS

You can't black-out the Stars

No. 19. Corvus (the Crow)

A southern constellation between Virgo and Hydra.

Education

A machine is a great moral educator. If a horse or a donkey won't go, men lose their tempers and beat it; if a machine won't go, there is no use beating it. You have to think and try till you find what is wrong. That is real education.

Professor GILBERT MURRAY

ELEGY ON THE DEATH OF A MAD DOG

GOOD people all, of every sort,
  Give ear unto my song ;
And if you find it wond'rous short,
  It cannot hold you long.

In Islington there was a man,
  Of whom the world might say,
That still a godly race he ran,
  Whene'er he went to pray.

A kind and gentle heart he had,
  To comfort friends and foes ;
The naked every day he clad,
  When he put on his clothes.

And in that town a dog was found,
  As many dogs there be,
Both mongrel, puppy, whelp, and hound,
  And curs of low degree.

This dog and man at first were friends ;
  But when a pique began,
The dog, to gain some private ends,
  Went mad and bit the man.

Around from all the neighbouring streets
  The wond'ring neighbours ran,
And swore the dog had lost his wits,
  To bite so good a man.

The wound, it seem'd both sore and sad
  To every Christian eye ;
And while they swore the dog was mad,
  They swore the man would die.

But soon a wonder came to light,
  That show'd the rogues they lied :
The man recover'd of the bite,
  The dog it was that died.

OLIVER GOLDSMITH

*　　　*　　　*

If a dog bites a man, that isn't news, but if a man
bites a dog, that's news !

LORD NORTHCLIFFE

Number, Please !

HERE are three more numerical problems for the quick-witted :

1. Three consecutive numbers below ten when added together produce a total equal to the square of the smallest number, less the amount of the largest.

2. If 5 is subtracted from a given number and what is left is subtracted from 120, the answer is four times the original number. What is the number ?

3. If five times 8 made 60, what would a quarter of 40 be ?

In case you're unable to solve them in the twinkling of an eye, you'll find the answers at the back of the book.

A—Zoo
No. 20. The Tiger

Tiger, tiger, burning bright
In the forests of the night,
What immortal hand or eye
Could frame thy fearful symmetry ?
                    WILLIAM BLAKE

Chestnut Corner
No. 2. Tunnel Trick

Lord Halifax is said, in his youth, while travelling by train, to have shared a carriage with two very prim-looking ladies. As the train passed through a tunnel, he kissed his own hand noisily several times and then, as he alighted at the next station, inquired gallantly : "To which of you charming ladies am I indebted for the delightful incident in the tunnel ?"

" Do you know, my mother-in-law's mouth is so large that when she opened it wide the other night a party of men began putting sandbags round it ! "

SPELLING A SQUARE

A GAME for quick wits and eyes is Spelling a Square. Any number of players may participate, and nothing more is needed than a piece of paper ruled like this to produce a six-by-six square.

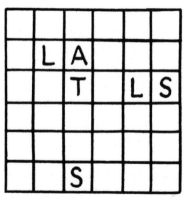

Now each player in turn calls out a letter which must immediately be entered up by every one participating in one of the small squares. The winner is the person who makes the greatest number of *bona fide* words during the game, which ends when all of the squares are full (*i.e.*, when thirty-six letters have been called out).

Scoring is as follows :

For a 6-letter word—5 marks.
For a 5-letter word—4 ,,
For a 4-letter word—3 ,,
For a 3-letter word—2 ,,
For a 2-letter word—1 mark.

Words should be made both horizontally and vertically, and the players should endeavour to call letters which will help their own prearranged words, but hinder their opponents.

In the square shown above, the — AT — — S might become CATERS, scoring 5 points, and the corresponding line across could be TOTALS, also scoring 5. If for any reason the player were unable to obtain the required letters for either word and finished with, say TOTALR and CATOQS, then 4 and 2 marks would be scored respectively.

If it is required to complicate the game still further, a non-playing announcer can read out letters at intervals of thirty seconds, leaving the players to make the best possible use of them.

Genius

The true genius says the wrong things at the right time.

C. G. JUNG

Strictly Personal

No. 19. Neville Chamberlain

Don't despair ! Keep the home fires burning !

It's a long Chamberlain that has no turning !

Odd Jobs

No. 3. Umbrella Library

A youngster in Brooklyn, New York, has built up a prosperous little business through hiring out umbrellas to passengers leaving the Underground on rainy days. There are no statistics to show how many of them are returned.

You can't black-out the Stars !

No. 20. Cygnus (the Swan)

This constellation lies in the most densely packed region of the Milky Way. Its brightest star (*Deneb Adige*) is that in the tail of the Swan.

7

Sickness *can* be an Asset

IF you have never been sick, never lost so much as a day in bed—then you have missed something ! When your turn comes, don't be dismayed. Remind yourself that pain and suffering may teach you something valuable, something that you could not have learned otherwise. Possibly it may change for the better the entire course of your life. You and those around you will be happier if you can look upon any illness as a blessing in disguise, and wisely determine to make the most of it. You *can* turn your sickness into an asset.

LOUIS E. BISCH

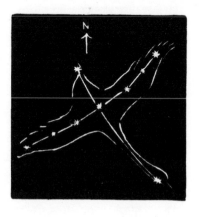

The Poetry of Love

Love is strong as death. Many waters cannot quench love, neither can the floods drown it.

PROVERBS

Robert Burns

O, my luve is like a red, red rose
  That's newly sprung in June :
O, my luve is like the melodie
  That's sweetly played in tune.

As fair thou art, my bonnie lass,
  So deep in luve am I :
And I will luve thee still, my dear,
  Till a' the seas gang dry.

Till a' the seas gang dry, my dear,
  And the rocks melt wi' the sun :
I will luve thee still, my dear,
  While the sands o' life shall run.

And fare thee weel, my only luve !
  And fare thee weel awhile !
And I will come again, my luve,
  Tho' it were ten thousand mile.

John P. Kemble

When first I attempted your pity
  to move,
    You seemed deaf to my sighs
    and my prayers ;
Perhaps it was right to dissemble
  your love,
    But why did you kick me down-
    stairs ?

P. B. Shelley

The fountains mingle with the
  river
  And the river with the Ocean,
The winds of Heaven mix for ever
  With a sweet emotion ;
Nothing in the world is single ;
  All things by a law divine
In one spirit meet and mingle,
  Why not I with thine ?

See the mountains kiss high Heaven
  And the waves clasp one an-
  other ;
No sister-flower would be forgiven
  If it disdained its brother ;
And the sunlight clasps the earth
  And the moonbeams kiss the sea :
What is all this sweet work worth
  If thou kiss not me ?

Robert Browning

    Escape me ?
    Never—
    Beloved !
While I am I, and you are you,
So long as the world contains us
  both,
Me the loving and you the loth,
While the one eludes, must the
  other pursue.

The Philosophy of Love

If there be no great love in the beginning, yet heaven may decrease it upon better acquaintance. . . . I hope on familiarity will grow more contempt.

SHAKESPEARE

Anatole France

In love, men demand forms and colours ; they *will* have visible images. Women only crave sensations. They love better than we ; they are blind. And if you say, But think of Psyche's lamp and the spilt drop of oil, I reply, Psyche does not represent woman. Psyche is the soul. It is not the same thing ; indeed it is just the opposite. Psyche was curious to see, and women are only curious to feel. Psyche was searching after the unknown ; when women search, it is never the unknown they are in quest of. They long to recover something lost, that is all—to recall something dreamt or something recollected, to renew some past sensation, nothing more. If they *had* eyes, how should we ever explain their loves ?

Heywood Brown

The ability to make love frivolously is the chief characteristic which distinguishes human beings from the beasts.

André Maurois

Every man worthy of the name puts his work before everything else in the world—even above the woman he loves. If she tries to lure him from his responsibilities so that he may devote himself entirely to her, he may allow it in the beginning, but not without acute remorse ; and the day will come when he will belong to the woman who puts more craft into her game.

The Common Man

Calf love, half love ; old love, cold love.

Nobody's sweetheart is ugly.

Of soups and love, the first is the best.

Love is like a sprain, the second time you get it more easily.

A man loves his sweetheart most, his wife best, and his mother longest.

Love enters man through his eyes, woman through her ears.

PYRAMID PATIENCE

ONE of the most baffling games of Patience I have ever tried is played with the eight weights belonging to the kitchen scales.

These are placed one on top of the other exactly as they are in the drawing.

Now stand the pile on top of a book or sheet of paper and place two more books or sheets of paper alongside.

All you are required to do is to move the pyramid of eight weights from Book No. 1 to Book No. 3, but with the following stipulations :

(a) You must move only one weight at a time.

(b) You must never place a heavier weight on top of a lighter.

To get a little practice, start with six weights only ; then work up to seven and eight. If you haven't a set of weights that fit into one another, like those in the illustration, cut out circles or squares of cardboard, in diminishing sizes, instead.

Now, just to start you off, here are the opening moves in one solution of the problem. I have used six weights only, and numbered the weights 1 to 6 in ascending order of size. (These moves are equally effective if you are using eight weights.)

Book I	Book II	Book III
123456	. .	. .
23456	. .	1
3456	2	1
3456	12	. .
456	12	3
1456	2	3
1456	. .	23
456	. .	123
56	4	123
56	14	23
256	14	3
1256	4	3

After that it should be easy— but wait till you try with eight !

A—Zoo

No. 21. The Skunk

I'm bound to say I'd funk
Calling a Skunk a skunk.

Chestnut Corner

No. 3. Tall Stories

Americans, like their sky-scrapers, are addicted to tall stories—like the one about the day when it was so hot that a dog chased a rabbit and they were both walking! Or about the man who thatched a barn on a foggy day and found, when the fog lifted, that he had inadvertently thatched ten feet beyond the barn.

" Okay, Toots ! "

The Idler

MUCH of the Pain and Pleasure of mankind arises from the conjectures which every one makes of the thoughts of others ; we all enjoy praise which we do not hear, and resent contempt which we do not see. The *Idler* may therefore be forgiven if he suffers his Imagination to represent to him what his readers will say or think when they are informed that they have now his last paper in their hands.

Value is more frequently raised by scarcity than by use. That which lay neglected when it was common, rises in estimation as its quantity becomes less. We seldom learn the true want of what we have till it is discovered that we can have no more.

SAMUEL JOHNSON

BLACK-OUT IN THE COUNTRY

(This perfect description of black-out in the country comes from Matthew Arnold's poem, " The Silent Friend.")

THE evening comes, the field is still ;
The tinkle of the thirsty rill,
Unheard all day, ascends again ;
Deserted is the new-reaped grain,
Silent the sheaves ! the ringing wain,
The reapers' cry, the dogs' alarms,
All housed within the sleeping farms !
The business of the day is done,
The last belated gleaner gone.
And from the thyme upon the height,
And from the elder-blossom white,
And pale dog-roses in the hedge,
And from the mint-plant in the sedge,
In puffs of balm the night-air blows
The perfume which the day forgoes ;
And on the pure horizon far,
See, pulsing with the first-born star,
The liquid sky above the hill !
The evening comes, the field is still.

Don't waste Matches!

THIS match problem is different from all the others. It offers you thirteen matches, arranged like this:

All you have to do is to take away one match and rearrange three others. The remainder must not be moved. If you do this correctly you will spell the word which is popularly supposed to be the *raison d'être* of all matches.

Strictly Personal
No. 20. J. B. Priestley

Priestley's finished doing time,
P'r'aps he'll next discover mime.
But I'm sure he can't afford an-
other Johnson over Jordan.

You can't black-out the Stars

No. 21. Andromeda
(the Chained Lady)

Named after the daughter of Cepheus and Cassiopeia, King and Queen of Ethiopia, this constellation contains Almach, a beautiful triple star.

Odd Jobs
No. 4. Fisherman's Friend

A Massachusetts resident, Mr H. P. Dovyard, sells worms to anglers in neat little cans, delivered like packets of cigarettes by a coin-in-the-slot automatic machine.

Associations

HERE are two lists of twelve words. Each of the words in the first list should inevitably be associated in your mind with one (and one only) of the words in the second list. Can you pair them off?

You should be able to put the right letter against all twelve numbers in less than a minute.

List One

1. Hamlet.
2. Football.
3. Derby.
4. Cadenza.
5. Robey.
6. Influenza.
7. Malaprop.
8. Belisha.
9. Isosceles.
10. Simon.
11. Iodine.
12. Cat.

List Two

A. Doctor.
B. Beacon.
C. Rivals.
D. Arsenal.
E. Exchequer.
F. Racing.
G. Triangle.
H. Shakespeare.
I. Lights.
J. Violin.
K. Variety.
L. Cut.

" *Say, mister, I've lost a sixpence. Did you see it along the road?* "

" *Well, now you come to mention it, sonny, I did notice a bit of a bump.* "

HOW IT FEELS TO BE BLIND

" It is not miserable to be blind ; it is miserable to be incapable of enduring blindness."—JOHN MILTON.

WHEN I consider how my light is spent,
　Ere half my days, in this dark world and wide,
And that one Talent which is death to hide,
Lodg'd with me useless, though my Soul more bent
To serve therewith my Maker, and present
My true account, lest He returning chide,
Doth God exact day-labour, light deny'd?
I fondly ask ; but Patience to prevent
That murmur, soon replies, God doth not need
Either man's work or his own gifts : who best
Bear his milde yoak, they serve him best; his State
Is Kingly.　Thousands at his bidding speed
And post o'er Land and Ocean without rest :
They also serve who only stand and waite.

JOHN MILTON, *On his Blindness*

Sensitive Similes

As subtle as the ' b ' in subtle.
J. A. SADLER

As silent as a sundial.
H. DE VERE STACPOOLE

As democratic as death.
RICHARD CONNELL

As dated as a calendar.
GEORGE JEAN NATHAN

As inquisitive as an X-ray.
H. C. WITWER

A—Zoo

No. 22. The Owl

The Owl is wise—
Look at his eyes !
He's worn pince-nez
For days and dez.

The General inspects the Balloons

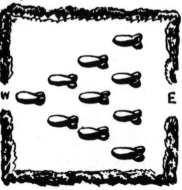

A FOREIGN general on a visit to England wanted to inspect the barrage balloons. In order to give him a closer look at them, ten balloons were lined up in a field, in a triangle with its point (or apex) facing the West gate, by which the general was expected to arrive. This is how they looked :

At the last moment the officer in charge of the balloons heard that the general was arriving by the East gate and that he must rearrange the balloons with the point of the triangle facing the other way. He managed to do this very quickly by moving only three balloons.

Can you do the same ?

Wisdom in Brief

Perhaps the time will come when mankind will honour its saviours more than its destroyers, Pasteur and Lister more than Napoleon and Ludendorff.

W. R. INGE

God made the sun and moon and stars, but man, his child, out of necessity made for himself lamplight as a beacon and a haven for the innermost secret of his heart.

GEORGE JEAN NATHAN

It is never any good dwelling on good-byes. It is not the being together that it prolongs, it is the parting.

ELIZABETH ASQUITH BIBESCO

It is most important in this world to be pushing, but it is fatal to seem so.

BENJAMIN JOWETT

The doctrine of human equality reposes on this : that there is no man really clever who has not found that he is stupid. There is no big man who has not felt small. Some men never feel small ; but these are the few men who are.

G. K. CHESTERTON

Bird and Beast

DID any bird come flying
After Adam and Eve,
When the door was shut against
    them,
    And they sat down to grieve ?

I think not Eve's peacock,
    Splendid to see.
And I think not Adam's eagle ;
    But a dove maybe.

Did any beast come pushing
    Through the thorny hedge ?
Into the thorny, thistly world,
    Out from Eden's edge ?

I think not a lion,
    Though his strength is such ;
But I think an innocent lamb
    May have done as much.
                    CHRISTINA ROSSETTI

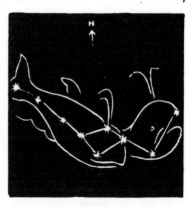

You can't black-out the Stars

No. 22. Cetus (the Whale)

A Southern constellation to the west of Orion.

Chestnut Corner

No. 4. World's Shortest Ghost Story

Although I knew I had locked the door, I felt instinctively that there was some one in the room. I reached for the matches. Some one put them into my hand.

Strictly Personal

No. 21. Lord Nuffield

*Meet the man who made the Motor pay
So he could give the money all away !*

LITTLE ONES OUT OF BIG ONES

DO you know what the back-woodsmen of the American Middle West call wood-chopping? Their name for it is " making little ones out of big ones."

Here's a game which has nothing to do with wood-chopping, but which has the same title.

All you need is a scrap of paper and a pencil. You can play it alone, for fun, or in a party for competition, forfeit, or prize.

First, take a word like DENOMINATION ; then see how many other words you can make out of the same letters. ' Den ' and ' nomination ' will strike you at once, but don't stop there. If you can't make more than twenty you must be very slow-witted.

Other useful words for this game are Disestablishment, Octogenarian, Evangelical, and Photographic, but there are hosts of others you can find for yourselves.

Kiddicorner

GEE UP !

WHAT'S wrong with these donkeys ?

Nothing but sheer laziness !

Turn to the back of the book and you'll see how they can be made to hurry without the slightest difficulty.

If you want to try this on somebody else, you can trace the donkeys quite easily with a piece of paper of medium thickness.

A GAME OF CHESS

SUPPOSE it were perfectly certain that the life and fortune of every one of us would one day or other depend upon his winning or losing a game of chess.

Don't you think that we should all consider it to be a primary duty to learn at least the names and the moves of the pieces ; to have a notion of a gambit and a keen eye for all the means of giving and getting out of check ? Do you not think that we should look with disapprobation amounting to scorn, upon the father who allowed his son, or the state which allowed its members, to grow up without knowing a pawn from a knight ?

Yet it is a very plain and elementary truth that the life, the fortune and the happiness of every one of us, and, more or less, of those who are connected with us, do depend upon our knowing something of the rules of a game infinitely more difficult and complicated than chess. It is a game which has been played for untold ages, every man and woman of us being one of the two players in a game of his or her own. The chess-board is the world, the pieces are the phenomena of the universe, the rules of the game are what we call the laws of Nature.   THOMAS H. HUXLEY

Epitaph for a Dog

In a New York pets' cemetery is a tombstone bearing the words :

JACK
AS EVER
PRECEDES HIS MASTER
BY A FEW STEPS

A—Zoo

No. 23. Ermine

*You must never mistake Ermine
For Vermin.*

How to tell if You're growing Old

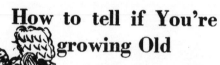

" A man is as old as he feels ;
a woman as old as she looks."

WE are all of us getting older every day, though few of us care to admit it. But old age is something every one should face up to. It isn't so much a matter of years, as of disposition, habit, and outlook. Many men of sixty and seventy are younger in outlook than their nephews of forty-five.

Here's an interesting little test for those on the shady side of forty.

Answer the following ten questions truthfully and then consult the key below to tell whether you are really getting old or not.

1. Do you feel that young people in the twenties are more foolish than you used to be at the same age ?

2. Do you like to have the same armchair in the same spot kept free for you always, and feel upset if some one else appropriates it ?

3. Do you think present-day children are precocious, noisy, ill-mannered, and disobedient ?

4. Do you begin to feel that going out to parties or the cinema is rather too much trouble and wish you could stay home by the fireside instead ?

5. Have you stopped reading the newspapers as carefully as you did ten years ago ?

6. Have you developed new ' fads ' about food or cooking in the past five years ?

7. Do you find that you no longer make friends as easily as you did ?

8. Have you become more intolerant, prejudiced, selfish, or lazy than you were ten years ago ?

9. Do you find that people you meet in business and social life are more dishonest and less likeable than they used to be ?

10. Do you find yourself thinking rather sadly about the ' good old days,' and forgetting how unhappy they often were ?

Now then, if you've answered all of those perfectly truthfully, we can tell a little more about you.

Seven or more answers of ' Yes ' mean that you're very definitely getting old ; four, five or six mean that you're at the dangerous point when old age is just round the corner, three or less betoken comparative immunity.

Whichever class you're in, the opposite page will tell you something about growing old gracefully.

How to grow Old Gracefully

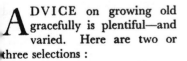
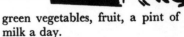

" Grow old along with me
The best is yet to be."—BROWNING

ADVICE on growing old gracefully is plentiful—and varied. Here are two or three selections :

Walter Pitkin

Slow down, but without giving up either career, work, or status.

Get out of the rut of routine into which people of marked ability in some speciality tend to sink.

Use your accumulated wisdom more and your muscles less.

Anticipate later years and the inevitable easing out of your career, which may be disastrous unless you create, well in advance of retirement, a set of new interests that may be pursued after sixty.

Keep in touch with the day's events, with the latest discoveries, and with the world's exciting trends, in order to continue sensitive and alert.

(From *Careers After Forty*.)

Lillian G. Genn

Have a physical examination at least once a year and follow the doctor's advice.

Eat balanced meals, including green vegetables, fruit, a pint of milk a day.

Take some form of light exercise daily, preferably walking.

Find time to relax, particularly at meal-time.

Get eight hours of sleep.

Control your weight.

Ride a hobby.

William Lyon Phelps

The best insurance against old age and disability is an interesting mind. I like to hang pictures on the walls of the mind ; I like to make it possible for a man to live with himself, so that he will not be bored with himself.

And here are a few thoughts on the compensations of old age.

Alonzo of Aragon

Old wood to burn !
Old wine to drink !
Old friends to trust !
Old authors to read !

Webster

Is not old wine wholesomest, old pippins toothsomest, old wood burns brightest, old linen wash whitest ? Old soldiers, sweethearts, are surest, and old lovers are soundest.

Fifteen and One

A NOTHER game which requires a great deal of patience, but which is so fascinating that, once you have begun it, you will be loath to go to bed without finishing it, is Fifteen and One.

For this you need a four-by-four square, like this, and 15 draughts pieces or scraps of cardboard numbered from one to fifteen. Shuffle these and place them on the board in any order. You will obviously have one square free. Now, the game is to move the pieces into the order given here, with the one blank square at the bottom right-hand corner.

To do this you may move any of the neighbouring pieces into blank square horizontally or vertically, *but not diagonally* (*i.e.*, you may move 12 or 15 into the blank square here, but not 11).

It sounds easy, doesn't it?

———

Odd Jobs

No. 5. Moth Merchant

I N Rochester, New York, lives one of the world's few moth merchants. He breeds and sells moths and butterflies—the latter for people who make 'butterfly-wing' lampshades and ornaments. Collectors patronize the moth merchant, too, and so do school teachers. He has a catalogue of about 400 kinds, half of them rare, and the prices range from sixpence to ten or fifteen shillings each.

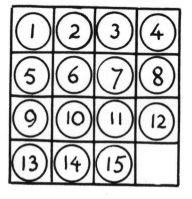

Jenny kiss'd Me

JENNY kiss'd me when
we met,
    Jumping from the chair
she sat in ;
Time, you thief, who love
to get
    Sweets into your list, put
that in !
Say I'm weary, say I'm sad,
    Say that health and wealth
have miss'd me,
Say I'm growing old, but
add,
    Jenny kiss'd me.
              LEIGH HUNT

(Did you know that
'Jenny' was Jane, the wife
of Thomas Carlyle ?)

You can't black-out the Stars

No. 23. *Bootes*
                  (the Herdsman)
    Situated next to Ursa Major,
this constellation contains Arcturus, the most swiftly moving of
all stars.

*   *   *

Chestnut Corner

No. 5. *Snub*
    A bore asked Oscar Wilde what
he should do about the conspiracy
of silence at that time affecting
his work. Wilde replied tersely :
" Join it ! "

*   *   *

Strictly Personal

No. 22. *H. G. Wells*
Can you wonder Wells looks glum,
Knowing the Shape of Things to
*   come ?*
Drawing a bow at a venture, he
Lives in the 21st Century.

8

More Associations

HERE is a harder set of associations.

Each of the names in List I should immediately associate itself in your mind with one of the names in List II.

If your brain is really alert you should be able to put the right letter against all of the numbers in sixty seconds.

Got your watch ready?

10. Cinema.
11. Juliet.
12. Lamp.

List II

A. Dancers.
B. Nightingale.
C. Whisky.
D. Balcony.
E. Turpin.
F. Gable.
G. Grace.
H. Christmas.
I. Bonaparte.
J. Cake.
K. Key.
L. Robin Hood.

List I

1. York.
2. Elba.
3. Twenty-one.
4. Cracker.
5. Wedding.
6. Green man.
7. Morris.
8. Walker.
9. Bat.

A—Zoo

No. 24. Hippopotamus

Hip—hip—hippopotamus!

Kiddicorner

Paper Patterns

THIS is nothing to do with the paper patterns Mother uses for her dressmaking—those odd-shaped scraps of buff-coloured flimsy given away inside women's magazines. This is a most artistic occupation for a long black-out evening — producing fascinating patterns like the one illustrated here.

The best plan is first to work out your design roughly on a piece of paper, so that you know just what you are about. Then take a sheet of newspaper— something of the more solid type, like *The Times*, is best for artistic pursuits like this—fold it very carefully, taking care that all of your folds are quite square, and tear it at the necessary points.

Done really well, paper patterns make an amusing decoration for

" *Where have you been all night, my lad ?* "

" *Handing provisions into the front-line trenches, sergeant—about 200 yards out there.*"

" *Good lord, man, that's the enemy front line !* "

" *Bli'me ! I thought you was all talking peculiar !* "

———

your bedroom or play-room, and you can have lots of fun making them to resemble your relatives and school friends.

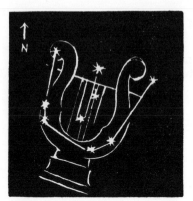

You can't black-out the Stars !

No. 24. *Lyra* (the Lyre)

A northern constellation containing Vega, Sleliak, and Sulaphat.

Chestnut Corner

No. 6. *Nothing but the Truth*

The captain and the mate kept the log during alternate weeks.

One day the captain wrote : " Mate was drunk to-day."

The mate protested ; said he had never been drunk before and had signed the pledge.

The captain said : " In this log we write the exact truth."

Next week the mate kept the log and wrote : " Captain was sober to-day."

The Special Constable's Beat

WHEN Mr Watkins, the bank manager, became a special constable, his first duty was to keep watch over six large factories. The sergeant told him he was to walk right round the outside of each factory, trying all the doors and keeping a look-out for anything suspicious. After two or three nights, he realized that he was retracing his steps several times, so next day at the bank he worked out a much shorter beat, which still fulfilled the sergeant's instructions to walk completely round each factory, but cut down the distance by more than one-third.

Can you work out the short beat ?

THE ENGLISH SUNDAY

THE most godlike thing in England is its Sabbath calm, for in what other way do we so surely ape divinity as in our seventh-day lassitude? God took His ease, and so do we. Can you imagine God—at any rate, such a God as made England, and that alone is a fair title even for heaven—can you imagine God dancing on a Sunday afternoon as Siva of the Hindus dances? Can you imagine Him joining a queue (the Milky Way) to see the Dioscuri, the Pleiades, Antares and the Snake, Arcturus and his precocious juvenile, or any other sidereal box-office attraction? God took His ease, and so does England. True, it may be necessary to relate some invasions of that ease; but they will not be related with any expression of approval. Six steps and a platform is the proper conception of a week, the ultimate step of Saturday night being steeper than the others.

ERIC LINKLATER

Strictly Personal

No. 23. Sir John Simon

NOT-SO-SIMPLE SIMON

Simple Simon
Met a pieman—
" Now that we're at war,"
  Said Simple Simon
  To the pieman,
" Life will cost you more."

Said the pieman
To Simple Simon :
" I have but one penny ! "
  Said Simple Simon
  To the pieman :
" Now you haven't any ! "

On Katherine Hepburn's performance in " The Lake "

" She ran the whole gamut of emotion from A to B."

DOROTHY PARKER

* * *

On the first performance of a new play called " The House Beautiful."

" The *House Beautiful* is the play lousy."

DOROTHY PARKER

* * *

On Tree's performance in " Hamlet."

" Funny without being vulgar."

W. S. GILBERT

* * *

On Frederic March's performance in " The Buccaneer."

" March comes in like a lion and goes out like a ham." [1]

FRANK NUGENT

* * *

On the first performance of a new play called " Dreadful Night."

" Exactly."

" THE TIMES."

* * *

On a new revue in New York.

" I have knocked everything except the knees of the chorus girls—and God anticipated me there."

PERCY HAMMOND

---

[1] *Ham :* Professional slang for bad actor.

The Critics have their Say . . .

Choice Flowers gathered from the bouquets presented by critics to plays and performers.

On a touring company in " Hamlet."

" Mr —— played the King as though in mortal fear some one was going to play the ace."

PROVINCIAL NEWSPAPER

* * *

On a Brahms concert.

" An amateur string quartet played Brahms here last evening. Brahms lost."

DETROIT NEWSPAPER

* * *

On Hollywood.

" Hollywood is the land of yes-men and acqui-yes girls."

DOROTHY PARKER

* * *

And the Author replies . . .

G. B. Shaw

At the first night of *Arms and the Man* when Shaw was acknowledging the applause, somebody in the gallery booed. Shaw at once replied with, " I quite agree with you, sir—but what are we two against so many ? "

* * *

J. R. Lowell

Nature fits all her children with
    something to do ;
He who would write and can't
    write can surely review.

Twist your Tongue on These!

HERE are four tongue-twisters for the whole family:

Sister Thelma thought three threads sufficient for sewing shirts for soldiers.

* * *

Fetch me a scuttle of sea coal in a school coal-scuttle.

* * *

Said the housewife to the tinker who was mending her saucepans:
"Are you copper-bottoming 'em?"

Said the tinker:
"No, I'm aluminiuming 'em, mum."

* * *

"The sixth sheep's sick," said the sixth son of the shepherd.

Voice of Sergeant: "*Oi! What are you doing?*"

Recruit: "*Sorry, sir, I'm a somnambulist.*"

Voice of Sergeant: "*I don't care what your religion is—you can't walk round the camp in your nightshirt!*"

A—Zoo

No. 25. The Eagle

Never take Beagles
To hunt Eagles.
NEW PROVERB

The Things They say
(without twisting their tongues)

Heredity is an omnibus in which all our ancestors ride, and every now and then one of them puts his head out and embarrasses us.

O. W. HOLMES

* * *

I get my exercise acting as pall-bearer to my friends who exercise.

CHAUNCEY DEPEW

* * *

I have a cure for boredom that will never fail. It is made up of ten rules: Go out among the people and perform one kind act ten times.

CARRIE CHAPMAN

NURSERY RHYMES

I love Sixpence

I love sixpence, pretty little sixpence,
  I love sixpence better than my life ;
I spent a penny of it, I spent another,
  And took fourpence home to my wife.

Oh, my little fourpence, pretty little fourpence,
  I love fourpence better than my life ;
I spent a penny of it, I spent another,
  And I took twopence home to my wife.

Oh, my little twopence, my pretty little twopence,
  I love twopence better than my life ;
I spent a penny of it, I spent another,
  And I took nothing home to my wife.

Oh, my little nothing, my pretty little nothing,
  What will nothing buy for my wife ?
I have nothing, I spend nothing,
  I love nothing better than my wife.

* * *

Four-and-Twenty Tailors

Four-and-twenty tailors went to kill a snail,
The best man among them durst not touch her tail ;
She put out her horns like a little Kyloe cow,
Run, tailors, run ! or she'll kill you all e'en now.

Dance to Your Daddie

Dance to your daddie,
My bonnie laddie,
Dance to your daddie, my bonnie lamb !
You shall get a fishie,
On a little dishie,
You shall get a herring when the boat comes hame !

Dance to your daddie,
My bonnie laddie,
Dance to your daddie, and to your mammie sing !
You shall get a coatie,
And a pair of breekies,
You shall get a coatie when the boat comes in !

* * *

Little Tommy Tittlemouse

Little Tommy Tittlemouse
Lived in a little house ;
He caught fishes
In other men's ditches.

* * *

Little Gossip

It costs little Gossip her income for shoes,
To travel about and carry the news.

YOU MAY NOT KNOW

In a Cottage in Fife

In a cottage in Fife
Lived a man and his wife
Who, believe me, were comical folk ;
For to people's surprise,
They both saw with their eyes,
And their tongues moved whenever
they spoke.

When they were asleep,
I'm told that to keep
Their eyes open they could not
contrive ;
They both walked on their feet,
And 'twas thought what they eat
Help'd, with drinking, to keep them
alive.

* * *

The King of France Went up the Hill

The King of France went up the hill
With twenty thousand men :
The King of France came down the
hill,
And ne'er went up again.

* * *

Bat, Bat

Bat, bat, come under my hat,
And I'll give you a slice of bacon,
And when I bake I'll give you a
cake,
If I am not mistaken.

Brow Brinky

Brow brinky,
Eye winky,
Chin choppy,
Nose noppy,
Cheek cherry,
Mouth merry.

* * *

Blue Eye, Grey Eye

Blue eye, beauty,
Grey eye, greedy,
Black eye, blackie,
Brown eye, brownie.

* * *

Pease Porridge Hot

Pease porridge hot,
Pease porridge cold,
Pease porridge in the pot,
Nine days old.
Spell me *that* without a P,
And a scholar you will be.

* * *

The Cat has ate the Pudding-string

Sing, sing, what shall I sing ?
The cat has ate the pudding-string !
Do, do, what shall I do ?
The cat has bit it quite in two !

Are You Certain?

HERE is another little brain-test with the answers considerately provided for you.

All you have to do is to decide which of the several possible answers given is the correct one.

1. The word 'Jerusalem' means ——

Holy City, abode of peace, Jewish home.

2. The Mufti is ——.

A Jewish tailor, a soldier in disguise, an Arab horseman, a Mohammedan theologian.

3. In Great Britain there is one Member of Parliament to every —— people.

20,000, 50,000, 65,000, 90,000.

4. In a three-shilling book of postage stamps there are —— 1½d. stamps.

8, 12, 18, 24.

5. There are —— feature films made every year.

208, 430, 580, 760, 1020.

6. The number of cinemas in Great Britain is ——.

2000, 3500, 5000, 7800.

7. There is one divorce in Great Britain to every —— marriages.

10, 26, 34, 60, 72.

8. The tallest tree in the world is the ——.

Poplar, coconut palm, eucalyptus, rubber.

9. The inhabitants of India speak —— different languages.

16, 86, 154, 220, 430.

10. Hara-kiri is ——.

A famous spy, a Chinese food, a Japanese suicide, a Mohammedan religion.

————

You can't black-out the Stars!

No. 25. *Pegasus*
(the Winged Horse)

One of the most ancient northern constellations, with Algenib and Scheat as its biggest stars.

The Sea hath its Pearls

THE sea hath its pearls,
   The heaven hath its stars ;
But my heart, my heart,
   My heart hath its love.

Great are the sea and the heaven ;
   Yet greater is my heart,
And fairer than pearls and stars
   Flashes and beams my love.

Thou little, youthful maiden,
   Come unto my great heart ;
My heart, and the sea, and the heaven,
   Are melting away with love !

H. W. LONGFELLOW

The Lift and the Stairs

It is a common saying that when prices go up in the lift, wages only ascend by the stairs ; but it is not always realized that when prices come down the lift, wages hold on to the banisters.

SIR JOHN SIMON

Strictly Personal

No. 24. James Agate

In the " Sunday Times " ce matin,
Agate writes of the stall he sat in,
The wine he drank and the weather
   that day,
Also en passant *about the play.*

Facing Both Ways

HAVE you tried building Palindromes?

No, Bobby, not Picturedromes! A Palindrome is a word or a sentence that reads exactly the same backward as forward.

There are several famous ones which you probably know. There's the Garden of Eden Palindrome to begin with. This goes like this:

"MADAM, I'M ADAM."

The first time Adam said that to Eve, he started a game that's been going on ever since.

Napoleon, for instance, after his downfall and internment on Elba, was asked whether he thought he could really have captured England as he had once threatened. The old Emperor replied:

"ABLE WAS I ERE I SAW ELBA."

Then there is the famous British one which goes like this:

"EGAD A BASE TONE DENOTES A BAD AGE."

If you go into some churches you will find a Palindrome running round the font, usually a very famous Greek one which goes like this:

NIΨONANOMHMAT
AMHMONANOΨIN

Now then, Bobby, you're learning Greek! What does it mean? You're not sure. Well, if I still remember my Greek, it's something like this:

"Wash my transgressions, not only my face."

The word Palindrome comes from the Greek, too, and means "to run back again."

You can make Palindromes out of initials, too, if you like. Here's a well-known one:

ETLNLTE

which translates as "Eat to live, not live to Eat."

Now suppose you all try your hands at building a Black-out Palindrome of your own. Then when you've finished it, you can send it along for me to see.

"Noon" is a good word to start with—or if the word which precedes it ends with 'e' you can have it read "No one" at the beginning. Have you got the idea? Then happy building to you!

A—Zoo

No. 26. The Dove

" This must be love ! "
Said the Turtle-dove.

Chestnut Corner

No. 7. The Psychiatrist

One day an American psychiatrist was introduced to Queen Marie of Rumania.

" This," said the person making the introduction, " is Queen Marie of Rumania."

" Really ? " said the psychiatrist absent-mindedly. " And how long has she had this idea ? "

" Bli'me ! where's the bloomin' ship ? "

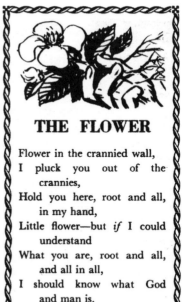

THE FLOWER

Flower in the crannied wall,
I pluck you out of the crannies,
Hold you here, root and all, in my hand,
Little flower—but *if* I could understand
What you are, root and all, and all in all,
I should know what God and man is.

TENNYSON

What Sort of Wedding?

I AM sure you all realize the importance of using the right adjective to describe anything you happen to be discussing. In fact, it is probably true to say that there are some adjectives which can only be applied to one word. Certainly that is true in a limited sense of the words printed below. The nouns in the first list, numbered 1 to 12, each need an adjective from the second list, marked A to L. Each adjective can reasonably apply to one noun and one only. Adjective G, for instance, can obviously only be placed with Noun 3. Can you put the appropriate letter against all the other numbers in less than sixty seconds?

First List
1. Fire.
2. Ember.
3. Wedding.
4. Earl.
5. Page.
6. Lips.
7. Track.
8. Sinner.
9. Word.
10. Law.
11. Mercy.
12. Seas.

Second List
A. Spoken.
B. Sealed.
C. Infinite.
D. Roaring.
E. Printed.
F. Unwritten.
G. Silver.
H. Miserable.
I. Belted.
J. High.
K. Glowing.
L. Beaten.

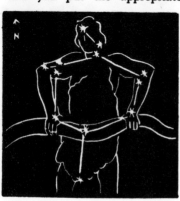

You can't black-out the Stars!

No. 26. Ophiuchus
(the Serpent-bearer)

Another of the oldest northern constellations, between Libra and Aquila.

Shaw says . . .

LIFE is no brief candle to me. It is a sort of splendid torch which I have got hold of for the moment, and I want to make it burn as brightly as possible before handing it on to future generations.

* * *

Man is a failure as a political animal.

* * *

Civilization is a disease produced by the practice of building societies with rotten material.

* * *

A moderately honest man with a moderately faithful wife, moderate drinkers both, in a moderately healthy house : that is the true middle-class unit.

* * *

The man with toothache thinks every one happy whose teeth are sound. The poverty-stricken man makes the same mistake about the rich.

* * *

Beware of the man whose god is in the skies.

* * *

The most anxious man in a prison is the governor.

* * *

Life levels all men ; death reveals the eminent.

Strictly Personal
No. 25. *George Bernard Shaw*
When our elders talk of Shaw,
Echo rudely answers : " Pshaw ! "

Jerome said about Shaw . . .

BERNARD SHAW'S name first became familiar to the general public as the result of scurrilous attacks, disguised as interviews, made upon him by a section of the London evening press. The interviewer would force his way into Shaw's modest apartment, apparently for no other purpose than to bully and insult him.

Many people maintained that Shaw must be an imaginary personage. Why did he stand it ? Why didn't he kick the interviewer downstairs ? Failing that, why didn't he call in the police ? It seemed difficult to believe in the existence of a being so Christian as this poor, persecuted Shaw appeared to be. Every one talked about him.

As a matter of fact, the interviews were written by Shaw himself.

On the Death of a favourite Cat

Drowned in a Tub of Goldfishes

On a favourite cat called Selima, that fell into a china tub with goldfishes in it, and was drowned. Walpole, after the death of Gray, placed the china vase on a pedestal at Strawberry Hill, with a few lines of the Ode for its inscription.

'TWAS on a lofty vase's side,
  Where China's gayest art had dy'd
  The azure flowers, that blow ;
Demurest of the tabby kind,
The pensive Selima, reclin'd,
  Gaz'd on the lake below.

Her conscious tail her joy declar'd ;
The fair round face, the snowy beard,
  The velvet of her paws,
Her coat, that with the tortoise vies,
Her ears of jet, and emerald eyes,
  She saw ; and purr'd applause.

Still had she gaz'd ; but 'midst the tide
Two angel forms were seen to glide,
  The Genii of the stream :
Their scaly armour's Tyrian hue
Through richest purple to the view
  Betray'd a golden gleam.

The hapless nymph with wonder saw
A whisker first, and then a claw,
  With many an ardent wish,
She stretch'd in vain, to reach the prize.
What female heart can gold despise ?
  What cat's averse to fish ?

Presumptuous maid !   with look intent,
Again she stretch'd, again she bent,
  Nor knew the gulf between.
(Malignant Fate sat by, and smil'd.)
The slipp'ry verge her feet beguil'd,
  She tumbled headlong in.

Eight times emerging from the flood
She mew'd to ev'ry wat'ry god,
  Some speedy aid to send.
Nor Dolphin came, nor Nereid stirr'd
Nor cruel Tom, nor Susan heard.
  A fav'rite has no friend !

From hence, ye beauties, undeceiv'd,
Know, one false step is ne'er retriev'd,
  And be with caution bold.
Not all that tempts your wand'ring eyes
And heedless hearts is lawful prize,
  Nor all that glisters, gold.

THOMAS GRAY

Dick Whittington's Cat was a Boat!

Feline History, Wisdom, and Verse

To a Cat

YOU may have seen Dick Whittington's cat in a panto-mime or a picture, but the original was really a boat.

In the fourteenth century, Norwegian boats, with narrow sterns and broad, deep waists, were used in the coal trade. Sometimes they were called ' cats,' and sometimes ' catches.'

Sir Richard Whittington, Lord Mayor of London in 1397, made his money trading in coal which he brought by ' cat ' from New-castle to London about 1381.

* * *

The Cheshire cat wasn't really a cat either, but a piece of cheese. In Cheshire, cheese was always sold moulded in the form of a cat, with a grinning mouth. So next time you're told you're " grinning like a Cheshire cat," you'll know you're being com-pared to a piece of cheese !

* * *

The trouble with the black-out, says my next-door neighbour, is that even the cats have no lights !

* * *

And an earlier savant re-marked that in the dark all cats are grey.

9

CAT ! who hast pass'd thy
    grand climacteric,
How many mice and rats hast
    in thy days
    Destroyèd ?—How many tit-bits
      stolen ? Gaze
With those bright languid seg-
    ments green, and prick
Those velvet ears—but pr'ythee
    do not stick
    Thy latent talons in me—and
      upraise
    Thy gentle mew—and tell me
      all thy frays
Of fish and mice, and rats and
    tender chick.
Nay, look not down, nor lick thy
    dainty wrists—
    For all the wheezy asthma—and
      for all
Thy tail's tip is nick'd off—and
    though the fists
    Of many a maid have given
      thee many a maul,
Still is that fur as soft as when
    the lists
    In youth thou enter'dst on
      glass-bottled wall.
          JOHN KEATS

———

" Cat and Fiddle," the name of many famous inns, really refers to Caton, a one-time Governor of Calais, who was known as Caton the Faithful, or Caton le Fidèle.

Kiddicorner

Run, Rabbit, run !

HERE'S a very easy way to make little rabbit marionettes. Cut out two pieces of material as illustrated here and sew them together. Add eyes,

mouth—beads are best for the eyes—then place one finger in each ear and double up the rest so that they help push out the rabbit's nose.

There ! Now you can arrange a little marionette dance to the tune of Noel Gay's jolly song, " Run, Rabbit, run ! "

He that hath not a dram of folly in his mixture hath pounds of much worse matter in his composition.

LAMB

A—Zoo

No. 27. Parrot

A cussed old parrot named Polly
  Allowed little things to incense her.
She always began with " By Golly ! "
  And the rest was cut out by the Censor.

" *I'm what you might call the sturdy oak type.*"
" *You may be sturdy, but I'm darned if you're oke.*"

This room looks rather untidy, doesn't it? Perhaps that's because it contains something beginning with every letter of the alphabet. Can you find all twenty-six?

Poets' Corner for Typists

Perfect Pairs

1. HOLIDAYS

She dives, she swims, she rides a horse,
She socks a golf ball round the course,
She plays a wicked tennis game,
She dances till she's nearly lame ;
And just when a romance is ripe—
The poor kid must revert to type.

2. RUSH HOUR

Under the tube-train's leather strap
  The homely maiden stands,
And stands and stands and stands and stands
  And stands and stands and stands.

ALL through history there have been pairs of names associated together because of love, hatred, friendship, or business. Here are the second halves of twelve famous pairs, ancient and modern, real or imaginary. Can you provide the other halves ?

1. —— and Joan.
2. —— and Cressida.
3. —— and Edgar.
4. —— and Andromeda.
5. —— and Jeff.
6. —— and Cleopatra.
7. —— and Hyde.
8. —— and Allen.
9. —— and Jonathan.
10. —— and Beatrice.
11. —— and Pollux.
12. —— and Mary.

Strictly Personal

No. 26. Viscount Gort

Viscount Gort
May be short
But he knows
The things he ought.

Chestnut Corner
No. 7. The Beer and the Tortoise

THREE tortoises went into a bar one day and ordered a beer apiece. Then they discovered they had no money.

So they elected the smallest tortoise to go back home and get the money ; but he was afraid that while he was gone, the others would drink his beer. They promised not to, so he went out and was gone two years.

Finally, the other tortoises got restless and one of them said to the other : " Don't you think he's not coming back, and we might drink his beer now ? "

Whereupon the little tortoise popped his head round the corner and cried :

" If you drink one drop, I won't go ! "

You can't black-out the Stars !

No. 27. Leo Minor
(the Little Lion)

A smaller constellation between Ursa Major and Leo Major.

A RAINY DAY

DOWN in a swift, tumultuous stream came the unwelcome rain to beat a sharp tattoo upon the patient window-pane. Umbrellas magically appeared as people hurried by. The children rushed in presently with loud, familiar cry : " Rain, rain, go away ! Come again another day ! " Only a nursery rhyme, yet what a foolish thing to say ! Without a drink the thirsty earth would be a sorry sight. No quickening green upon the bough, no meadows to invite ; no paddly pools to play in ; no rainbows in the sky. The days in endless sunshine would languidly drift by. So Nature sends the rain, and sunshine follows after. Our lives are much the same, first tears and then the laughter.

Do You know?

THINK-ING CAPS on, please!

No, father, not that one!

Here are six straightforward, simple, general-knowledge questions. How many can you answer?

1. What are the names of the Seven Seas you hear so much about?

2. Who says, "Who goes home?" and why?

3. What is a caret, and what is it used for?

4. What happened to John Brown whose body, according to the song, "lies a-mouldering in the grave"?

5. Why are the Prime Minister and his immediate associates called "the Cabinet"?

6. What is the name of the projectile used instead of a ball in ice-hockey?

A—Zoo

No. 28. The Otter

Most Zoos have got a Otter.

Odd Jobs

No. 6. Shoe-breaker-inner

Martha Mitchel, of New York, runs a thriving business which will break in a pair of shoes for any customer for something between ten shillings and a pound. She has employees with feet of all sizes, and these break in about fifty pairs of shoes a week. Hardest to please, apparently, are the women who buy shoes half a size too small for them.

Speak in French only when you can't think of the English for a thing.

LEWIS CARROLL

" I still think we should have turned left! "

Kiddicorner

Take Five Lines!

ONCE upon a time there were two boys sitting next to each other at school. They looked rather like this :

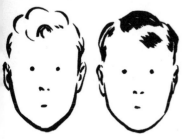

Perhaps they were talking to each other, or giggling, or doing something they shouldn't. At any rate, the master said to each of them, " Take five lines ! "

His words had quite a different effect on the two boys. The five lines made one look cheerful and one look glum—just like this :

Amusing, isn't it ?

Now, if you think you can improve on these, trace the first designs on to a piece of plain paper and see what you can do with just five lines !

A Song about Myself

THERE was a naughty Boy,
  And a naughty Boy was he,
He ran away to Scotland
  The people for to see—
    Then he found
    That the ground
    Was as hard,
    That a yard
    Was as long,
    That a song
    Was as merry,
    That a cherry
    Was as red—
    That lead
    Was as weighty,
    That fourscore
    Was as eighty,
    That a door
    Was as wooden
    As in England—
So he stood in his shoes
  And he wonder'd,
  He wonder'd,
He stood in his shoes
  And he wonder'd.
        JOHN KEATS

They wrote This

Byron

TO-MORROW is my birthday; that is to say, at twelve o'clock midnight, *i.e.*, in twelve minutes, I shall have completed thirty and three years of age ! ! !—and I go to my bed with a heaviness of heart at having lived so long, and to so little purpose.

It is three minutes past twelve—" 'Tis the middle of the night by the castle clock," and I am now thirty-three.

> *Eheu, fugaces, Postume, Postume,*
> *Labuntur anni ;—*

but I don't regret them so much for what I have done, as for what I *might* have done.

> *Through life's road, so dim and dirty,*
> *I have dragged to three-and-thirty.*
> *What have these years left to me :*
> *Nothing—except thirty-three.*

Fanny Burney

August, 1786. An attempt has just been made upon the life of the king ! I was almost petrified with horror at the intelligence. If this king is not safe—good, pious, beneficent as he is—if his life is in danger from his own subjects, who is to guard the throne ? And which way is a monarch to be secure ?

Mrs Goldsworthy had taken every possible precaution so to tell the matter to the Princess Elizabeth as least to alarm her, lest it might occasion a return of her spasms ; but, fortunately, she cried so exceedingly that it was hoped the vent of her tears would save her from those terrible convulsions.

William Makepeace Thackeray

Carillon. I was awakened this morning with the chime which Antwerp Cathedral clock plays at half-hours. The tune has been haunting me ever since, as tunes will. You dress, eat, drink, walk, and talk to yourself to their tune : their inaudible jingle accompanies you all day : you read the sentences of the paper to their rhythm. I tried uncouthly to imitate the tune to the ladies of the family at breakfast, and they say it is " the shadow dance of *Dinorah* ! " It may be so. I dimly remember that my body was once present during the performance of that opera, whilst my eyes were closed, and my intellectual faculties dormant at the back of the box ; howbeit I have learned that shadow dance from hearing it pealing up ever so high in the air at night, morn, noon.

in Their Diaries

Stefan Lorant

1st July, 1933 (*I was Hitler's Prisoner*). The key creaked in the lock. It was the warder opening the door of the cell.

"Get up! Fetch your water!" he called out. Morning had come; a new day had dawned.

"Write a novel last night?" Strachwitz asked, in a bantering tone.

"I couldn't sleep. I've been writing down all sorts of nonsense."

"Well, you'd better tear it up, then, in case anyone finds it in your possession."

"I shall do nothing of the kind."

Strachwitz shook his head.

"I'm afraid one of these fine days you'll be 'shot while trying to escape,' if you don't give up your scribbling."

I did not answer. I knew he was right. If my notes were found on me, it would mean death. It was high time I got my diary out of the prison. But how?

Arthur Koestler

16th February, 1937 (*Spanish Testament*). The walls of this cell were beautifully white and unsullied, and provided an extensive surface upon which to write. A piece of wire from my bedstead once more served me for pencil. I also began to scrawl my diary on the wall, but I stuck over it. As long as I was thinking them out, my sentences seemed quite sensible, but no sooner had I begun to scribble them down than I fell as though bewitched into the sentimental penny-novelette style.

Arnold Bennett

11th December, 1927 (*Journal*). Mrs P. Campbell came for tea at 5.30 and made a terrific outpouring. She said: "If you want to keep me quiet, give me a cigar." So I gave her one. Later, she went out into the Square smoking it. Her energy seems quite unimpaired. She now wants to produce and play in *Flora*. She arrived with a great scheme all complete. She read the play about a year ago or more, and saw nothing in it. Now she reads it again and sees everything in it.

Kiddicorner

How to make a ' Rubber ' Stamp

WOULD you like to have a rubber stamp with your name or personal design on it for the modest cost of an evening's work?

Here's one way in which you can do so.

First, forget all about rubber and use an oblong piece of linoleum instead. Using a razor blade in one of those ingenious holders which prevent your cutting yourself, cut out the design or the letters of your name (which should, of course, be drawn first in pencil or ink to give you an exact guide).

When you have finished, glue or tack the linoleum to a piece of wood of the same area and half an inch thick. Then beg or borrow one of those small doorknobs with a screw end and fasten this neatly in the centre of the wood.

The most important thing of all I have left till the last. Your name—or the design you choose—must, of course, be reversed on the linoleum if it is to give the right result when you use the stamp. To obtain this result, print your name carefully on a thin piece of paper, reverse this, and use it to trace your name on the linoleum. And you won't forget that you must cut away all of the surface *except* the outline of the letters, will you?

Strictly Personal

No. 27. Charlie Chaplin

Talkies blare from North and South but
He knows when to keep his mouth shut.

Hymn of Hate

The chore which makes me very
    sore
  And is no cause for laughter,
Is madly scrubbing out the tub
  Before my bath and after.
    Col. ROBERT WOOD, *Knowledge*

You can't black-out the Stars !

No. 28. Lacerta (the Lizard)

A small constellation in the
Milky Way, between Cygnus and
Andromeda.

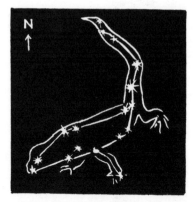

THE DEVON MAID

WHERE be ye going, you Devon Maid ?
    And what have ye there in the basket ?
Ye tight little fairy just fresh from the dairy,
  Will ye give me some cream if I ask it ?

I love your meads, and I love your flowers,
  And I love your junkets mainly,
But 'hind the door I love kissing more,
  O look not so disdainly.

I love your hills, and I love your dales,
  And I love your flocks a-bleating—
But O, on the heather to lie together,
  With both our hearts a-beating !

I'll put your basket all safe in a nook,
  Your shawl I hang up on the willow,
And we will sigh in the daisy's eye
  And kiss on a grass green pillow.
                JOHN KEATS

THE WIDOW'S PEARLS

ONCE upon a time there was an old widow who had three nieces, Mary, Marjorie, and May—and a valuable string of 19 pearls.

When she died, it was found that she had given instructions in her will for the pearls to be divided between the nieces in the following proportions:

> Mary—one-half.
> Marjorie—one-quarter.
> May—one-fifth.

The three girls puzzled their heads over the division of the pearls for hours and then, quite unable to find any way of dividing 19 by 2, 4 or 5, went to see the aunt's solicitor about it.

He smiled, and solved the problem for them in five minutes. Can you suggest how he did it?

A—Zoo

No. 29. The Duck

The wise man looked at the quacking Duck—
He looked at it long and frowned.
" How is it," he said, " when its legs are so short,
That they reach down to the ground?"

———

" The children's boat-pond? Yes, lady—you go past the trenches, turn to the left by the searchlight, carry on till you get to the gas-mask stores, and it's just beyond the barrage balloon."

MY WIFE AND I

Jan. 12. This evening I observed my wife mighty dull, and I myself was not mighty fond, because of some hard words she did give me at noon, out of a jealousy at my being abroad this morning, which, God knows, it was upon the business of the Office unexpectedly ; but I to bed, not thinking but she would come after me. But waking by and by, out of a slumber, which I usually fall into presently after my coming into the bed, I found she did not prepare to come to bed, but got fresh candles, and more wood for her fire, it being mighty cold, too. At this being troubled, I after a while prayed her to come to bed ; so, after an hour or two, she silent, and I now and then praying her to come to bed, she fell into a fury, that I was a rogue and false to her. I did, as I might truly, deny it, and was mightily troubled, but all would not serve. At last, about one o'clock, she came to my side of the bed, and drew my curtain open, and with the tongs red hot at the ends, made as if she did design to pinch me with them, at which, in dismay, I rose up, and with a few words, she laid them down ; and did by little and little, very sillily, let all the discourse fall ; and about two, but with much seeming difficulty, come to bed, and there lay well all night, and long in bed talking together, with much pleasure, it being, I know, nothing but her doubt of my going out yesterday, without telling her of my going, which did vex her, poor wretch !

SAMUEL PEPYS (*Diary*)

MIXED BAG

HERE is a mixed bag of puzzles, problems, conundrums, and queries for you all to try out on one another.

1. Which comes first — the Hunter's Moon or the Harvest Moon?

2. If you went into a post office with a letter and a parcel, the postage on which added up to 1s. 1d., and the parcel cost a shilling more than the letter, how much would the letter cost?

3. To which poet does the description " neat sonnet or deep tearful lay " best apply?

4. My first measures time, my second spends time, my whole passes the night alone with it. Who am I?

5. Which are the world's largest continent, longest river, largest ocean, and longest railway tunnel?

6. What are camel-hair brushes made of?

7. What happened when NAT SIL went courting NAN FILD?

8. Add one vowel to this as often as you like and it should produce an illuminating motto:
  TOBPRFCTPRSVR.

9. What is the normal way of saying that " the construction in bricks and mortar of Mussolini's capital was not achieved in a single revolution of the earth upon its axis " ?

10. Can you spell ' insomnia ' with five ' S-s ' ?

A—Zoo

No. 30. Camel

The Dromedary's got the hump
Because of the Camel's extra hump.

You can't black-out the Stars

No. 29. Lepus (the Hare)

A southern constellation, to the south of Orion and east of Canis Major.

Stand up and work !

Have you heard about the manufacturer who had a band play " God Save the King " all day in his plant to prevent a sit-down strike ?

A Cat in Distress

A CAT in distress,
Nothing more, nor less ;
Good folks, I must faithfully
tell ye,
As I am a sinner,
It waits for some dinner
To stuff out its own little
belly.

You would not easily guess
All the modes of distress
Which torture the tenants of
earth ;
And the various evils,
Which, like so many devils,
Attend the poor souls from
their birth.

Some a living require,
And others desire
An old fellow out of the way ;
And which is the best
I leave to be guessed,
For I cannot pretend to
say.

One wants society,
Another variety,
Others a tranquil life ;
Some want food,
Others, as good,
Only want a wife.

But this poor little cat
Only wanted a rat,
To stuff out its own little
maw ;
And it were as good,
Some people had such food,
To make them *hold their
jaw* !

P. B. SHELLEY

PROVERBS OF TO-DAY—

Jewels five-words long,
That on the stretched forefinger of all time
Sparkle for ever.   TENNYSON

MONEY lost, nothing lost.
Courage lost, much lost.
Honour lost, more lost.
Soul lost, all lost.

*

Make your plans for the year at its beginning ; correct your wife from the first day.

*

Plenty is the child of peace.

*

It is a poor heart that never rejoices.

*

Experience is a precious gift, only given a man when his hair is gone.

*

A father is a banker given by Nature.

*

A nickname is the hardest stone that the devil can throw at a man.

*

A beggar can never be bankrupt.

*

Mockery is often poverty of wit.

As the sands of the desert are to the weary traveller, so is over-much speech to him that loveth silence.

*

Many feel dejected after pleasures, banquets, and public holidays.

*

Ducks lay eggs ; geese lay wagers.

*

Wartime Proverb

He that tilleth his land shall have plenty of bread.

PROVERBS

A good drum does not need hard striking.

*

All sorrows are bearable if there is bread.

*

God will not seek thy race,
  Nor will He ask thy birth ;
Alone He will demand of thee,
  What hast thou done on earth ?

*

Until death, all is life.

*

Seest thou a man that is hasty in his words ? There is more hope of a fool than of him.

*

Open rebuke is better than secret love.

—AND YESTERDAY

*A Proverb is the wit of one man
and the wisdom of many.*
EARL RUSSELL

Children's children are the crown of old men ; and the glory of children are their fathers.

★

Wealth maketh many friends, but the poor is separated from his neighbour.

★

A fool and his money are soon parted.

★

Enough is as good as a feast.

★

A merry heart doeth good like a medicine.

★

Speech is silver, silence is gold.

★

Two of a trade seldom agree.

★

Examine what is said, not him who speaks.

★

Beauty is a good letter of introduction.

10

Beware of desperate steps. The darkest day,
Live till to-morrow, will have passed away.

★

Follow pleasure, then will pleasure flee !
Follow duty—and pleasure will follow thee.

★

> **Judicial Proverb**
>
> *The Courts of Justice are open to all—so is the Ritz.*
>
> LORD DARLING

A word spoken in due season, how good is it !

★

Wisdom : her ways are ways of pleasantness,
And all her paths are peace.

★

'Tis good to be merry and wise ;
'Tis good to be honest and true ;
'Tis good to be off with the old love,
Before you are on with the new.

Do you use Long Words ?

HAVE you a friend who likes to use long words, whether he knows what they mean or not ?

If so, try these out on him. They are quoted by authorities as being the longest in existence.

Nitrophenylenediamine.

This little fellow—a mere 21 letters—was used by Sir William Crookes in describing one of the many chemical products on which he worked.

Then there is

Deanthropomorphization

which runs one letter ahead of the other ; but both of these pale into insignificance beside

Llanfairpwllgwyngyllgogerychw-yrndrobwllllandyssiliogogogoch.

This is a Welsh village in Anglesea which contains almost as many letters in its name as houses in its streets. There are actually 59 of them, if I've re-membered it correctly. Count them for yourselves if you don't believe me ! But if you write to anyone there, just use the first 20 or 30—the postman will know what you mean !

Then, if you're interested in metaphysics, you can talk about the

Inanthropomorphizability

of deity, and if you look at a certain line in Shakespeare's *Love's Labour's Lost* you'll find

Honorificabilitudinitatibus.

But really, all of these are quite short beside the really long words, one of which—I wouldn't inflict it on any printer !—consists of 179 letters and 78 syllables. Sanskrit, they say, goes one better still, with a word of 152 syllables !

You can't black-out the Stars

No. 30. Monoceros
(the Unicorn)

This constellation is south of Cancer and Gemini.

Letter to a Little Girl

Matthew Prior to Lady Margaret Cavendish Holles-Harley, when a child.

MY noble, lovely, little Peggy,
Let this my First Epistle beg ye,
At dawn of morn, and close of even,
To lift your heart and hands to Heaven.
In double duty say your prayer:
Our Father first, then *Notre Père*.
And, dearest child, along the day,
In every thing you do and say,
Obey and please my lord and lady,
So God shall love and angels aid ye.

If to these precepts you attend,
No second letter need I send,
And so I rest your constant friend—

MATTHEW PRIOR

Strictly Personal

No. 28. Somerset Maugham

*No need to inform
Mr Somerset Maugham
That it no longer pays
A chap to write plays.*

Chestnut Corner

No. 7. Observer observed

A scientist, observing the habits of a small monkey, tried to make the monkey play with a bat and ball. The monkey steadfastly refused to do so.

So the scientist decided to leave the little creature alone in the room with the bat and ball. He closed the door and waited a moment. Then, very silently, he stooped and peered through the keyhole into the monkey's room.

He found himself staring into an intent brown eye.

Is your Brain working?

HERE are three of the easiest possible problems, all depending on a careful reading of the question and summing up of its implications. Can you see through all three?

1. An old man died leaving £3000. His will directed that this money should be paid over to two mothers and two daughters. But it also directed that none of them should have less than £1000. How could his wishes be carried out?

2. If Big Ben takes exactly four seconds to strike four, how long will it take to strike midnight?

3. The last one is in verse—which ought to make it easier (to remember !) :

If five times four made thirty-three,

What would a fifth of fifty be?

* * *

Patience

Too many people see in patience merely a passive virtue, a waiting, a hoping. Patience also means sustained effort.

ANDRÉ MAUROIS

You can't black-out the Stars!

No. 31. Pisces
(the Southern Fish)

The Southern Fish contains one bright star—the Fomalhant, or Fish's Mouth.

Odd Jobs

No. 7. Ladies of the Navy

SWEDISH girls have the blood of centuries of seamen in their veins, and many of them train as sailors.

Two fine sailing ships, similar in design to those used by us for training cadets, are devoted to the teaching of these ladies of the navy.

The girls work hard, suffer tired muscles and sore hands, and jump to it even when the bos'n's whistle calls them from their hammocks in the middle of the night. And when they return to Stockholm, tired, sunburned, fit, and thoroughly at home with the workings of a ship, they must sit for an examination in things nautical.

THE WISH

WELL, then ! I now do plainly see
    This busy world and I shall ne'er agree.
The very honey, of all earthly joy
Does of all meats the soonest cloy ;
And they, methinks, deserve my pity,
Who for it can endure the stings,
The crowd and buzz and murmurings
    Of this great hive, the city.

Ah, yet, ere I descend to the grave
May I a small house and large garden have ;
And a few friends, and many books, both true,
Both wise, and both delightful too !
And since love ne'er will from me flee,
A mistress moderately fair,
And good as guardian angels are,
    Only beloved and loving me.

ABRAHAM COWLEY

A—Zoo

No. 31. The Cow

The friendly Cow, all red and white,
  I love with all my heart :
She gives me cream with all her might,
  To eat with apple-tart.
R. L. STEVENSON

Talking of Cows

If the Almighty wanted milk pasteurized He would have put a pasteurizing apparatus in the cow.
REEVE ALLAN CALDWELL

There was a Young Lady of —

The best limericks are unprintable, so—

IT was just as I thought it
      would be—
I sat next the Duchess at tea.
   Her rumblings abdominal
   Were simply phenomenal
And every one thought it was me !

* * *

A man went to drive in the
      black-out,
But first through the gate he'd to
      back out ;
   He chose the wrong gear
   And believe me, my dear,
Right through his own house he
      went smack out.

* * *

There was an old lady of Crewe
Who hurried to catch the 2.2.
   Said the porter, " Don't hurry,
   Or worry, or flurry—
It's a minute or 2222."

* * *

There was a young fellow of
      Twickenham,
Who bought some new shoes and
      walked quick in 'em.
   He trudged half a mile
   Till he came to a stile—
Then took off his shoes and was
      sick in 'em.

There was a young man of Japan,
Whose poetry never would scan.
   When his friends asked him why,
   He would simply reply :
" Well, you see, I always try to
      get as many feet into the
      last line as I possibly can ! "

* * *

Young folk who frequent picture
      palaces
Have no use for psycho-analysis.
   Although Dr Freud
   Used to get most annoyed,
They still cling to their long-
      standing fallacies.

* * *

There was a young Lady of Ryde
Who ate bitter apples and died.
   The apples fermented
   Inside the lamented,
Making cider inside her inside.

* * *

There was a faith-healer of Deal,
Who said, " Although pain isn't
      real,
   If I sit on a pin
   And it punctures my skin
I dislike what I fancy I feel."

There was a Young Man of —

—I've had to print the best I know.

THERE was a young man of
St Bee's
Who thought he was stung by a
wasp.
    When they said, " Does it
    hurt ? "
    He replied, " Not a bit—
I thought all the time it was a
hornet."

* * *

There was a young man on a
yacht
Who said : " Though it's terribly
hacht,
    I won't eat an ice,
    For though ice is nice,
To say that it's cooling is racht ! "

There was a young lady of
Riga,
Who smiled as she rode on a
tiger.
    They returned from the ride
    With the lady inside,
And the smile on the face of the
tiger.

* * *

There was a young woman named
Bright,
Who travelled much faster than
light.
    She started one day
    In a relative way
And returned on the previous
night.

THE PELICAN

A peculiar bird is the Pelican,
His mouth can hold more than his
    belly can,
    He will hold in his beak
    Enough food for a week,
But I never can see how the hell he can.

You've often quoted It !

BUT HAVE YOU EVER READ THE WHOLE POEM?

TO A MOUSE

WEE, sleekit, cow'rin',
    tim'rous beastie,
Oh, what a panic's in thy
    breastie !
Thou need na start awa' sae
    hasty,
  Wi' bickering brattle !
I wad be laith to rin an' chase
    thee,
  Wi' murdering prattle !

I'm truly sorry man's dominion
Has broken Nature's social
    union,
An' justifies that ill opinion,
  Which makes thee startle
At me, thy poor, earth-born
    companion,
  An' fellow-mortal !

I doubt na, whiles, but thou
    may thieve ;
What then ? poor beastie, thou
    maun live !
A daimen-icker in a thrave
  'S a sma' request :
I'll get a blessin' wi' the lave,
  And never miss't !

Thy wee bit housie, too, in
    ruin !
Its silly wa's the win's are
    strewin' !
An' naething, now, to big a
    new ane,
  O' foggage green !
An' bleak December's winds
    ensuin',
  Baith snell an' keen !

Thou saw the fields laid bare
    an' waste,
An' weary winter comin' fast,
An' cozie here, beneath the
    blast,
  Thou thought to dwell,
Till, crash ! the cruel coulter
    pass'd
  Out through thy cell.

That wee bit heap o' leaves an'
    stibble,
Has cost thee mony a weary
    nibble !
Now thou's turn'd out, for a'
    thy trouble,
  But house or hald,
To thole the winter's sleety
    dribble,
  An' cranreuch cauld !

But, Mousie, thou art no thy
    lane,
In proving foresight may be vain:
The best laid schemes o' mice
    an' men
  Gang aft a-gley,
An' lea's us nought but grief
    an' pain,
  For promis'd joy.

Still thou art blest, compar'd
    wi' me !
The present only toucheth thee:
But, Och ! I backward cast
    my e'e
  On prospects drear !
An' forward, tho' I canna see,
  I guess an' fear !
          ROBERT BURNS

The Magic Square

TAKE the figures from 1 to 9 and write them down in three lines of three, like this :

```
1   2   3
4   5   6
7   8   9
```

Now rearrange the figures so that whichever way you add up the lines—horizontally, vertically, or diagonally—the answer will always be the same.

How to furnish a Dug-out

There are several schools of thought as to the way a dug-out should be furnished. At the moment my own view inclines to : A wireless set, a tinned tongue, a bottle of whisky, a box of cigars, a pack of cards, a volume of Damon Runyon.

JAMES AGATE

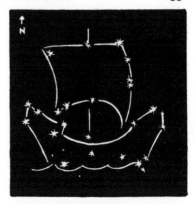

You can't black-out the Stars

No. 32. Navis argo
(the Good Ship *Argo*)

The largest constellation in the heavens.

Chestnut Corner

No. 8. *Chinese Credit*

The following sign recently appeared outside a Chinese laundry :

You want credit,
Me no give—
You get sore.
You want credit,
Me give,
You no pay—
Me get sore.
Better you get sore.

A—Zoo

No. 32. *The Squirrel*

" *Nuts to you !* " said the Squirrel.

The Man who hoarded Petrol

WHEN petrol rationing came in recently there was one foolish fellow who thought he could hoard petrol in an old tin drum in his garden.

Apart from the fact that this was a very dangerous thing to do, and against the law, there was the difficulty that the drum leaked. In fact, it leaked so badly that if the motorist put in two gallons during the day—which was all he could carry home in a small can—exactly one gallon of it leaked away during the night.

If the tank held eight gallons, and he went on putting in two gallons every day—and if one leaked away every night—how long would it be before the tank was quite full ?

Officer : " *Who are you ?* "
Scots recruit : " *Nae sae bad, sir. Hoo's yersel' ?* "

A—Zoo

No. 33. The Swan

One thing I know about a Swan—
Its young is never called a suckling.
The Cygnet as it swims behind
Its mamma's just an Ugly Duckling.
And by the way, here's another thing—
Did you ever see a Cygnet on a ring ?

The Things They say

Perhaps the principal objection to a quarrel is that it interrupts an argument.

G. K. CHESTERTON

* * *

Other people are quite dreadful. The only possible society is oneself.

OSCAR WILDE

* * *

Suspicion is very often a useless pain.

Dr JOHNSON

* * *

We are as much inclined to underrate our possibilities as to overrate our achievements.

Dean INGE

You can't black-out the Stars
No. 33. Vulpecula
(the Little Fox)

Sometimes called the Fox and the Goose, this northern constellation lies between Delphinus and Cygnus.

GOOD-NIGHT

GOOD-NIGHT? Ah! no; the hour is ill
  Which severs those it should unite;
Let us remain together still,
  Then it will be *good* night.

How can I call the lone night good,
  Though thy sweet wishes wing its flight?
Be it not said, thought, understood—
  Then it will be—*good* night.

To hearts which near each other move
  From evening close to morning light,
The night is good; because, my love,
  They never *say* good-night.

P. B. SHELLEY

By their Surnames shall ye know Them

Have you ever noticed how many characters there are in history who would never be recognized by any of us if it were not for their distinctive surnames, second names, or places of origin?

How many of the Christian names can you fill in on the list below?

1. —— of Aragon.
2. —— o' Groats.
3. —— the Tyler.
4. —— of Perth.
5. —— of Gaunt.
6. —— à Kempis.
7. —— of Hexham.
8. —— à Becket.
9. —— of Troy.
10. —— of Cleeves.

You can't black-out the Stars

No. 34. *Delphinus* (Dolphin)

A small constellation due east of Aquila.

A—Zoo

No. 34. The Hedgehog

At school the Hedgehog never shines,
Except when it comes to writing lines.

Do you know What goes on Inside—?

OUR restless hive is preparing to swarm. In obedience to the order of the hive spirit, 60,000 or 70,000 bees out of the 80,000 or 90,000 that form the whole population will abandon the maternal city at the prescribed hour. They do not leave it because food is lacking. No, were the hive poor, had it suffered from pillage or storm, had misfortune befallen the royal family, the bees would not forsake it. They leave it only when it has attained the apogee of its prosperity. Never is the hive more beautiful than on the eve of its heroic renouncement. Let us endeavour to picture it to ourselves, not as it appears to the bees—for we cannot tell in what magical, formidable fashion things may be reflected in the 6000 or 7000 facets of their lateral eyes—but as it would seem to us, were we of their stature. From the height of a dome more colossal than that of St Peter's at Rome, waxen walls descend to the ground, balanced in gigantic and geometric constructions, to which, for relative precision, audacity, and vastness, no human structure is comparable. Each of these walls, whose substance still is immaculate and fragrant, contains thousands of cells that are stored with provisions sufficient to feed the whole people for several weeks. Here, lodged in transparent cells, are the pollens, love-ferment of every flower of spring, making brilliant splashes of red and yellow, of black and mauve. Close by, in twenty thousand reservoirs, sealed with a seal that shall only be broken on days of supreme distress, the honey of April is stored, most limpid and perfumed of all. Still lower the honey of May matures in great open vats, by whose side watchful cohorts maintain an incessant current of air. In the centre, the warmest part of the hive, there stands the abode of the future—the royal domain of the brood-cells. Finally, in the holy of holies of these parts, are the three, four, six, or twelve sealed palaces, vast in size compared with the others, where the adolescent princesses lie who await their hour, wrapped in a kind of shroud, and fed in the darkness.

MAURICE MAETERLINCK
(*The Life of the Bee*)

> *How doth the little busy bee*
> *Improve each shining hour,*
> *And gather honey all the day*
> *From every opening flower.*

Music hath Charms—

Music hath charms to soothe the savage breast,
To soften rocks, or bend a knotted oak.

CONGREVE

Shelley

MUSIC, when soft voices die,
    Vibrates in the memory—
Odours, when sweet violets sicken,
Live within the sense they quicken.

Rose leaves, when the rose is dead,
Are heaped for the beloved's bed ;
And so thy thoughts, when thou art gone,
Love itself shall slumber on.

William Cowper

We keep no bees, but if I lived in a hive I should hardly hear more of their music. All the bees in the neighbourhood resort to a bed of mignonette, opposite to the window, and pay me for the honey they get out of it by a hum, which, though rather monotonous, is as agreeable to my ear as the whistling of my linnets. All the sounds that Nature utters are delightful—at least in the country.

★

Byron

There be none of Beauty's daughters
    With a magic like to thee ;
And like music on the waters
    Is thy sweet voice to me :
When, as if its sound were causing
The charmed ocean's pausing,
The waves lie still and gleaming,
And the lull'd winds seem dreaming :
And the midnight moon is weaving
    Her bright chain o'er the deep ;
Whose breast is gently heaving,
    As an infant's sleep :
So the spirit bows before thee,
To listen and adore thee ;
With a full but soft emotion,
Like the swell of Summer's ocean.

★

Herrick

Charm me asleep, and melt me so
    With thy delicious numbers,
That, being ravish'd, hence I go
    Away in easy slumbers.
    Ease my sick head,
    And make my bed,
Thou power that canst sever
    From me this ill,
    And quickly still,
    Though thou not kill
        My fever.

—The Poets say

*Music is a kind of inarticulate un-
fathomable speech, which leads us to
the edge of the infinite, and lets us for
moments gaze into that.*

CARLYLE

Tennyson

There is sweet music here that
softer falls
Than petals from blown roses
on the grass,
Or night-dews on still waters
between walls
Of shadowy granite, in a gleaming pass ;
Music that gentlier on the spirit
lies,
Than tired eyelids upon tired
eyes ;
Music that brings sweet sleep
down from the blissful skies.

★

Sebastian Evans

A blue robe on their shoulder,
And an ivory bow in hand,
Seven fiddlers came with their
fiddles
A-fiddling through the land,
And they fiddled a tune on their
fiddles
That none could understand.

Shakespeare

The man that hath no music in
himself,
Nor is not mov'd with concord
of sweet sounds,
Is fit for treasons, stratagems, and
spoils ;
The motions of his spirit are dull
as night,
And his affections dark as
Erebus :
Let no such man be trusted.

If music be the food of love, play
on.
Give me excess of it ; that, sur-
feiting,
The appetite may sicken, and so
die.
That strain again ;—it had a
dying fall :
O, it came o'er my ear like the
sweet sound
That breathes upon a bank of
violets,
Stealing and giving odour.

✷

Thomas Fuller

Music is nothing else but wild
sounds civilized into time and
tune. Such the extensiveness
thereof, that it stoopeth so low as
brute beasts, yet mounteth as
high as angels.

Make Your own Stencils

A STENCIL with which you can decorate all your own possessions— and particularly your own books— can be very easily made from waxed paper or thin cardboard. To obtain the best results the paper or card should be pinned to a board and the lettering or design very carefully drawn.

If you are using lettering, see that it is equally spaced on either side of a middle line drawn from top to bottom of the card, and that all of the letters sit squarely on top of lines drawn parallel to one another across the card.

Now take a pen-knife with a sharp point, or a razor-blade in a holder (never use a razor-blade without a holder), and cut out the stencil. You know, of course, that with letters you must leave ' ties,' or small pieces of card, in place to hold such portions of the card as the centre of the letter ' O,' and you can see from the drawing on this page how to do the same for a design.

When your stencil is made, you will be able to use it with water-

colour dabbed on by means of a stencil brush, or a small pad of cloth.

———

Who wrote It?

Crabbèd Age and Youth
Cannot live together :
Youth is full of pleasance,
Age is full of care ;
Youth like summer morn,
Age like winter weather ;
Youth like summer brave,
Age like winter bare.
(*Nobody knows, although some scholars attribute it to Shakespeare*)

You can't black-out the Stars!

No. 35. Draco (the Dragon)

One of the best-known northern constellations, containing Juza, Thuban, Tais, and Alwaid.

Women, Wine, and Snuff

Give me women, wine, and snuff
Until I cry out, " Hold, enough ! "
You may do so *sans* objection
Till the day of resurrection ;
For, bless my beard, they aye
    shall be
My beloved Trinity.

JOHN KEATS

A—Zoo

No. 35. The Sole

*The Sole has no feet and
therefore no sole. Poor soul !*
II

Odd Jobs
No. 8. Monkey Nuts

IN certain parts of Africa the monkey is taking the place of both human and machine labour in the harvesting of the coconut crop.

For several years the yield of coconuts has been so abundant that the negroes, though not troubled by the limitations of an eight-hour day, have been unable to handle it adequately.

They conceived the idea of training monkeys to gather the coconuts, and so successful were their efforts that the men's work paled into insignificance in comparison with that of their simian assistants.

At the same time, a new profession has made its appearance in darkest Africa—that of monkey trainer.

DRINKING

THE thirsty earth soaks up the rain,
*   And drinks, and gapes for drink again;*
The plants suck in the earth, and are
With constant drinking fresh and fair;
The sea itself (which one would think
Should have but little need of drink)
Drinks twice ten thousand rivers up,
So fill'd that they o'erflow the cup.
The busy Sun (and one would guess
By's drunken fiery face no less)
Drinks up the sea, and when he's done,
The Moon and Stars drink up the Sun:
They drink and dance by their own light,
They drink and revel all the night:
Nothing in Nature's sober found,
But an eternal health goes round.
Fill up the bowl, then, fill it high,
Fill all the glasses there—for why
Should every creature drink but I?
Why, man of morals, tell me why?

ABRAHAM COWLEY

Bookworm's Pilgrimage

WHEN a library was packing up its most valuable books to take them to a place of safety a few weeks ago, one of the curators found that a bookworm had been at work on a set of four volumes of history. The worm had made its way from the first page of the first volume to the last page of the fourth volume as they stood in their usual places on the shelves.

If each volume was an inch thick and each cover a quarter of an inch thick, how far had the bookworm travelled?

A—Zoo

No. 36. The Pony

The Pony never goes out to play,
When they ask him to, he just says,
" Neigh ! "

You can't black-out the Stars !

No. 36. Eridanus (the River)

A southern constellation, just below Taurus.

Chestnut Corner

No. 9. Likee?

The Chinese have a great reputation for politeness — but politeness of their sort can be a most effective weapon against blunderers.

As witness the British politician who made the mistake of asking a Chinese diplomat at dinner :

" You likee more wine, yes ? "

The guest thanked him politely —and a few moments later replied to a toast in perfect English. As he sat down he turned to his neighbour and said :

" You likee speechee, yes ? "

Bright Thoughts from Evacuees

With evidences of evacuation on all sides the " Black-Out Book " presents a distilled selection of schoolboy howlers. Why, by the way, are howlers always

' Evacuation ' is what the sun does to water.

*

Hell hath no fury like a woman's corn.

*

A horticulturalist is a man of culture who spoils himself by being haughty.

*

A passive verb is one in which the subject is the sufferer, such as " He was married to her."

The Buffalo was invented to stop trains.

The future tense of " He is drinking " is " He is drunk."

*

" Courting disaster " means when a man gets engaged.

*

Giraffes and ostriches need long necks because their heads are so far from their bodies.

*

I think Parnell was wrong and Gladstone was right. I have no reason for saying this.

*

No one has yet succeeded in spitting an atom.

*

Cæsar was warned to be careful of the Ideas of Frederic March.

*

Crops grow best where the ground is futile.

The Things that Teachers hear

attributed to boys ? Do girls never blunder ? For further examples of juvenile wit, the reader is referred to the collections of Mr Cecil Hunt.

A *pas seul* is something wrapped up in brown paper and string.

*

A panorama is a sort of hat worn in South America.

> ## Moral
>
> A youth should not be made to hate study before he know the causes to love it : or taste the bitterness before the sweet ; but called on, and allured, entreated and praised : Yea, when he deserves it not.
>
> BEN JONSON

" Arguing in a circle " means a round-table conference.

*

An antiquarian is a man who drinks nothing but water.

A Republican is the same as a sinner.

*

A blue stocking is something mother uses to make clothes whiter.

*

Life insurance was first introduced in order to pay funeral expenses.

*

A Bison is something to be sick into.

One at a Time

PERHAPS the simplest of all puzzles and certainly one of the most fascinating is making word ladders. These consist of a number of words all of the same length and each varying in only one letter from those above and below them. The purpose of the ladder is to change one word into another, and the winner is the player whose ladder contains the smallest number of rungs.

A well-known example is the ladder from SHOE to BOOT, which you will see for yourself goes like this :

```
S H O E
S H O T
S O O T
B O O T
```

Of course each intervening word (each rung of the ladder) must be found in the dictionary. Not all ladders are as short as the instance given above—sometimes you need a long ladder and a great deal of ingenuity to get to your goal—but you will find them all fascinating and tantalizing.

Here are a couple of examples for which you will find the answers in the back of the book.

1. Turn BIND into LANE.

And then a harder one :

2. Turn BLACK into WHITE.

A—Zoo

No. 37. *The Snake*

The trouble with the Baby Snake
Is that he simply won't sit up straight.

You can't black-out the Stars !

No. 37. *Equuleus* (the Foal)

A small constellation midway between Pegasus and Aquarius.

Short Story

There were many ardent suitors for her hand. And they sent her orchids and violets, and lilies and roses. All save one, a poor young fellow, who sent her but a simple little bunch of daisies.

She married the man who sent orchids.

GEORGE JEAN NATHAN

Preserving the Traditions

WOMAN

WHEN lovely woman stoops to folly,
And finds too late that men betray,
What charm can soothe her melancholy ?
What art can wash her tears away ?

The only art her guilt to cover,
To hide her shame from ev'ry eye,
To give repentance to her lover,
And wring his bosom is —to die.

OLIVER GOLDSMITH

Strictly Personal
No. 29. Dr Cronin

The stars look down on Dr Cronin
And hear a most unhappy moanin'
From specialists in Harley Street.
" A doctor shouldn't tell ! " they
bleat.

A—Zoo
No. 38. The Greyhound

> *Greyhounds all hate a*
> *Totalizator.*

It's on the Tip of My Tongue !

NOW then, family, do you know the answers to these very simple questions ?

1. How did shrapnel get its name ?

2. What is the origin of the word ' lynching ' ?

3. Which race in the world has the highest birth-rate ?

4. How many degrees are there in a right angle in England ?

5. Is it the same number in Germany ?

6. About how many words are there in an unabridged English dictionary ?

7. How many different words are used in the Bible (Authorized Version) ?

8. What is a taste bud ?

9. How much of the world's food supply is eaten by insects ?

10. If a man lives to be seventy, how long has he spent shaving, washing, and dressing ?

Bright Boy?

IS your child going to be bright, or the sort that makes howlers? If you want to tell early in life, watch for these signs. The bright child will have : marked desire for knowledge, retentive memory, great range of general information, and early speech. He (or she) will ask intelligent questions, have keen observation and an unusual vocabulary, expressive reading, good ear for music, be quick with figures, like to copy pictures and enjoy repairing things.

You can't black-out the Stars !

No. 38. Hydra (the Sea-serpent)

The longest of the southern constellations, containing altogether about 400 stars visible to the naked eye.

Diversion on a Penny Whistle

AWAY with Systems ! Away with a corrupt World ! Let us breathe the air of the Enchanted Island. Golden lie the meadows : golden run the streams ; red gold is on the pine-stems. The sun is coming down to earth, and walks the fields and the waters.

The sun is coming down to earth, and the fields and the waters shout to him golden shouts. He comes, and his heralds run before him, and touch the leaves of oaks and planes and beeches lucid green, and the pine stems redder gold ; leaving brightest footprints upon thickly weeded banks, where the foxglove's last upper-bells incline, and bramble-shoots wander amid moist rich herbage. The plumes of the woodland are alight ; and beyond them, over the open, 'tis a race with the long-thrown shadows ; a race across the heaths and up the hills, till, at the farthest bourne of mounted eastern cloud, the heralds of the sun lay rosy fingers and rest.

GEORGE MEREDITH

Looking back on Shakespeare

Matthew Arnold

John Dryden

OTHERS abide our question. Thou are free.

We ask and ask—Thou smilest and art still,

Out-topping knowledge. For the loftiest hill,

Who to the stars uncrowns his majesty,

Planting his steadfast footsteps in the sea,

Making the heaven of heavens his dwelling-place,

Spares but the cloudy border of his base

To the foil'd searching of mortality ;

And thou, who didst the stars and sunbeams know,

Self-school'd, self-scanned, self-honour'd, self-secure,

Didst tread on earth unguess'd at.—Better so !

All pains the immortal spirit must endure,

All weakness which impairs, all griefs which bow,

Find their sole speech in that victorious brow.

HE was the man who, of all Modern and perhaps Ancient Poets, had the largest and most comprehensive soul. All the Images of Nature were still present to him, and he drew them, not laboriously, but luckily; when he describes anything you more than see it, you feel it too. Those who accuse him to have wanted learning give him the greater commendation : he was naturally learned ; he needed not the spectacles of Books to read Nature ; he looked inwards, and found her there. I cannot say he is everywhere alike ; were he so, I should do him injury to compare him with the greatest of Mankind. He is many times flat, insipid ; his Comick wit degenerating into clenches, his serious swelling into Bombast. But he is always great when some great occasion is presented to him ; no man can say he ever had a fit subject for his wit and did not then raise himself high above the rest of poets.

Shakespeare's Fault

I REMEMBER, the Players have often mentioned it as an honour to *Shakespeare*, that in his writing (whatsoever he penned) he never blotted out line. My answer hath been, would he had blotted a thousand. Which they thought a malevolent speech. I had not told posterity this, but for their ignorance, who choose that circumstance to commend their friend by, wherein he most faulted; and to justify mine own candour (for I loved the man, and do honour his memory (on this side Idolatry) as much as any). He was (indeed) honest, and of an open and free nature: had an excellent *Phantasie*; brave notions, and gentle expressions: wherein he flowed with that facility, that sometime it was necessary he should be stopped: his wit was in his own power; would the rule of it had been so too. Many times he fell into those things, could not escape laughter: As when he said in the person of *Caesar*, one speaking to him; *Caesar did never wrong, but with just cause*: and such like; which were ridiculous. But he redeemed his vices with his virtues. There was ever more in him to be praised than to be pardoned.—BEN JONSON.

You can't black-out the Stars!

No. 39. Cepheus (the Monarch)

A northern constellation named after the King of Ethiopia, husband of Cassiopeia and father of Andromeda. Its brightest stars—Alrai, Alphirk, and Alderamin—are of third magnitude.

A—Zoo

No. 39. The Giant Panda

"The Giant Panda is the greatest money-maker the London Zoo has ever had."—Newspaper report.

Wait till the postman tries to hand a Tax-demand to the Giant Panda.

More Conjuring Tricks

THIS second selection of conjuring tricks is a little more advanced than that given earlier in the book, but anyone can perform them with a little practice.

Choose your Number

Take a small piece of paper, write the figure 9 on it, fold it, and place it in your pocket. Now take another piece of paper and, in the presence of your victim, write the figures 294 on it. Hand the pencil to your victim and ask him to cross out one of the figures. Almost always he will cross out the 9, and you can then produce the paper from your pocket to prove that you ' willed ' him to do so.

But supposing he crosses out the 2 or the 4 ? Easy ! Ask him to cross out a second figure. If he then chooses the 4 or the 2, you produce the paper bearing—quite remarkably —the number he rejected. And if he crosses out the 9 at the second attempt, you simply tell him that his will-power is too strong for you— which will please him mightily !

Sugar is Scarce

As long as sugar is rationed you may have to perform this trick with nuts, or some other objects—but

for the purposes of explanation we will assume that you are using sugar.

You take two lumps, but take care to let the audience think you

have only one. The first you hold prominently between the thumb and finger of your left hand ; the second you keep hidden inside the left hand. Now place the first lump in your mouth, make a few flourishes, and produce it again (actually it's Lump No. 2, of course) from your left ear. Exhibit this lump and pretend to take it with your right hand, while actually palming it in your left. Place your right hand, still clenched as though it contained the sugar, on top of your head and then pretend to rub the sugar into your head. Show

---

PATTER

Half the effect of a conjuring trick—perhaps more than half— depends on the breeziness of your patter. Talk hard all the time you are doing a trick—talk to make your audience laugh—talk to make them miss the little substitution or manipulation that might give the game away—talk to make the trick appear more difficult—and then talk !

---

the right hand, now empty (as it has been all the time, of course) and then extract Lump No. 1 from your mouth.

Half an hour's practice in front of a mirror will make this appear a very difficult trick.

Cutting a Hole in a Handkerchief

Perhaps you've seen a conjurer take a pocket handkerchief in his clenched hand, pull the middle of it through the tiny circle made by his

for Black-out Nights

clenched forefinger and thumb, and then, to the accompaniment of gasps from the audience, cut off the protruding piece with a pair of scissors? And perhaps you've seen him repair the hole with apparent ease? Well, here's a way in which you can do the same.

You procure a piece of white cloth similar to the material of the handkerchief and hide this in your palm before picking up the handkerchief. When you apparently pull the centre of the handkerchief through and cut it off, it is actually the other piece of

but with a hole cut out of the middle. After cutting off the portion of cloth, you produce the property handkerchief and exhibit it to prove that you have actually spoiled the handkerchief. Later, you palm this and produce the borrowed handkerchief, quite unharmed.

Repairing the Tears in Paper

This appears an inexplicable trick to people seeing it for the first time, but actually it is amazingly easy.

Take two exactly similar pieces of tissue paper. Fold one piece into a little wedge and tuck one corner of it behind a signet ring worn on the left hand, so that it is hidden from view in the palm of the hand.

Now take the other piece, exhibit it to the audience, and ask somebody to tear it into four or five pieces.

As soon as the pieces are handed back to you, roll them up into a ball and dispose of them in any way that appears effective. You can use one of those exciting looking top hats (after it has been examined by the audience) or any other container.

Actually, of course, all you do is conceal the little ball of torn pieces and produce the exactly similar piece from behind your signet ring.

cloth you are maltreating. Now take the scrap of cloth you have cut off and rub it back into your fist (actually palming it as you do so) reciting meanwhile the necessary 'magic' words to make it rejoin the handkerchief. Then all you have to do is to produce the handkerchief, quite whole and unharmed.

When you have a little more experience of palming, you can improve the trick by having a property handkerchief exactly similar to the one you use for the trick (the latter should be borrowed from the audience to add to the comic effect)

When you become a little more accomplished, you can do without the signet ring and palm the second piece of paper, or conceal it in your clothes.

Strictly Personal

No. 30. Hugh Walpole

How we would love to see Hugh Walpole
Sitting on the top of an awfully tall pole.

Odd Jobs

No. 9. Ahead in the Clouds

Just a score of young women have the job of air hostess.

They fly day after day in giant air-liners, attending to the comfort of lady passengers ; dispensing tea, advice, and cheerfulness to every one aboard who needs it. A girl who hasn't got her head in the clouds can get ahead in the clouds.

A—Zoo

No. 40. The Penguin

The Penguin never fails
To dress in tails.

A CHILD

A CHILD'S a plaything
for an hour ;
Its pretty tricks we try
For that or for a longer
space—
Then tire, and lay it by.

But I knew one that to itself
All seasons could control ;
That would have mock'd
the sense of pain
Out of a grieved soul.

Thou straggler into loving
arms,
Young climber-up of
knees,
When I forget thy thousand
ways,
Then life and all shall
cease.

MARY LAMB

Letter Logic

WHICH letter of the alphabet is used the most?

Almost anyone knows that—the answer, of course, is ' E.'

But do you know any more than that about the number and use of letters? Here are a few questions to try out on yourself and the rest of the family.

1. After ' e,' which are the three most-used letters in the English language?

2. Which are the three letters used least?

3. What is the proportion of vowels to consonants in English?

4. Which are the most-used initial letters in English?

5. Which are used least as initial letters?

6. Which are the most common letters at the ends of words?

7. Which letters make words by themselves?

8. Which are the most common two-letter words?

9. And the most common three-letter words?

You can't black-out the Stars!

No. 40. Aquila (the Eagle)

Situated in the Milky Way, almost due south of Lyra.

Analysis of Wars

AFTER analysing 902 wars and 1615 internal disturbances of the past 2500 years, a Harvard professor has decided that the nation with the most warlike record is Spain, which has been at war for over 67 per cent. of her history.

Runners-up, he says, are : Greece, 57 per cent. ; England, 56 per cent. ; France, 50 per cent. ; Russia, 46 per cent. ; and Italy, 36 per cent. Germany comes last of the big European nations, having been at war only during 28 per cent. of its history. How times change !

Kiddicorner

LET'S MAKE UP!

A MIRROR, a burnt cork, a few pieces of black paper, and you can have lots of fun making up your faces into all sorts of unusual characters. (Luckily, it all washes off again afterwards!)

Little pieces of black paper, cut to the right size and stuck on to one's teeth can make the prettiest faces look comic.

Dabs of burnt cork in the shapes shown in this drawing produce the perfect clown.

And perhaps the best fun of all is the set of orange-peel teeth. This drawing shows you how they are cut out—and how they look when you put them in place. (Better than Claude Dampier, isn't it?)

Later on, when you go in for acting, perhaps you will be able to persuade Father and Mother to give you a make-up box, so that you can assume more advanced disguises.

A—Zoo
No. 41. The Mongoose

Mon goose must be a peculiar bird—
It never lays eggs, so I have heard.

Variety's the Spice of Life!

A cinema in Alaska has shown only one film for ten years, a 'Wild Western' (silent), made in 1928. The theatre is open once a week, and the Eskimo customers will have no other picture. The owner has already worn out eight prints of the film.

You can't black-out the Stars!

No. 41. Auriga (the Waggoner)

The feature of this constellation is the great double-star, Capella.

The Grasshopper and the Cricket

THE poetry of earth is never dead:
　　When all the birds are faint with the hot sun,
And hide in cooling trees, a voice will run
From hedge to hedge about the new-mown mead;
That is the Grasshopper's—he takes the lead
In summer luxury—he has never done
With his delights; for when tired out with fun
He rests at ease beneath some pleasant weed.
The poetry of earth is ceasing never:
On a lone winter evening, when the frost
Has wrought a silence, from the stove there shrills
The Cricket's song, in warmth increasing ever,
And seems to one in drowsiness half lost,
The Grasshopper's among some grassy hills.

JOHN KEATS

Artful Anagrams

THOSE of you who have solved crossword puzzles will know all about anagrams. (There aren't any crossword puzzles in this book, by the way, because I thought you would find all you wanted of them in your daily papers.) An anagram is a word made by taking all of the letters of another word and rearranging them.

All of the words in a Palindrome are anagrams, of course, so we'll take a couple out of our own Palindromes, as examples, shall we?

Take the letters of ELBA, rearrange them, and you have ABLE. Or take WAS and rearrange it to make SAW.

Of course, an anagram need not necessarily have the letters in the same order, as with these examples. They can be entirely rearranged or transposed into any order. For instance, MELON is the anagram of LEMON.

Here are a few easy examples for you to start on. See if you can find anagrams for—

    1. USE.

    2. SMITE.

    3. TILL.

    4. ROSE.

    5. ARREST.

    6. PACES.

If you can't, you'll find the answers at the back of the book.

A—Zoo

No. 42. The Llama

Llamas
All wear striped pyjamas.

Men with Power

IF I had to select four men who have had more power than any others, I should mention Buddha and Christ, Pythagoras and Galileo. No one of these four had the support of the State until after his propaganda had achieved a great measure of success. No one of the four had much success in his own lifetime. No one of the four would have affected human life as he has done if power had been his *primary* object. No one of the four sought the kind of power that enslaves others, but the kind that sets them free—in the case of the first two, by showing how to master the desires that lead to strife, and thence to defeat slavery and subjection; in the case of the second two, by pointing the way towards control of natural forces.

BERTRAND RUSSELL

You can't black-out the Stars!

No. 42. *Crater* (the Cup)

A southern constellation, to the south of Leo and Virgo, named after its likeness to a two-handled drinking-cup.

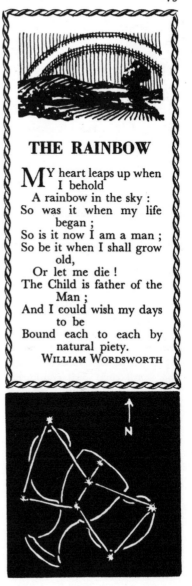

THE RAINBOW

MY heart leaps up when I behold
  A rainbow in the sky :
So was it when my life
    began ;
So is it now I am a man ;
So be it when I shall grow
    old,
  Or let me die !
The Child is father of the
    Man ;
And I could wish my days
    to be
Bound each to each by
    natural piety.

WILLIAM WORDSWORTH

I WROTE A LETTER
TO MY LOVE

Henry VIII to Anne Boleyn

MINE own Sweet-heart,—This shall be to advertize of the great elengeness that I find here since your departing ; for, I assure you, me thinketh the time longer since your departing now last than I wont was to do a whole fortnight. I think your kindness and my fervency of love causeth it, for otherwise I would not have thought it possible that for so little a while it should have grieved me. But now I am coming toward you, methinketh my pains be half relieved ; and also I am right well comforted, insomuch that my book maketh substantially for my matter. In token whereof I have spent above four hours this day, which hath caused me now to write the shorter letter to you at this time, because of some pain in my head ; wishing myself specially one evening in my sweetheart's arms, whose pretty dukkys I hope shortly to kiss. Written by the hand of him that was, is, and shall be yours by his own will.

Thomas Gray to Horace Walpole

(with a copy of his " Elegy ")

DEAR SIR,—As I live in a place, where even the ordinary tattle of the town arrives not till it is stale, and which produces no events of its own, you will not desire any excuse from me for writing so seldom, especially as of all people living I know you are the least a friend to letters spun out of one's brains, with all the toil and constraint that accompanies sentimental productions. I have been here at Stoke a few days (where I shall continue good part of the summer) ; and having put an end to a thing, whose beginning you have seen long ago, I immediately send it to you. You will, I hope, look upon it in the light of a *thing with an end to it* ; a merit that most of my writings have wanted, and are like to want, but which this epistle I am determined shall not want, when it tells you that I am ever,

Yours,

T. GRAY.

A LETTER FROM MARGATE

William Cowper to Rev. W. Unwin

(*July*, 1779)

WHEN I was at Margate, it was an excursion of pleasure to go to Ramsgate. The pier, I remember, was accounted a most excellent piece of stonework, and such I found it. By this time, I suppose, it is finished; and surely it is no small advantage, that you have an opportunity of observing how nicely those great stones are put together, as often as you please, without either trouble or expense. But you think Margate more lively. So is a Cheshire cheese full of mites more lively than a sound one : but that very liveliness only proves its rottenness. I remember, too, that Margate, though full of company was generally filled with such company, as people who were nice in the choice of their company, were rather fearful of keeping company with. The hoy went to London every week loaded with mackerel and herrings, and returned loaded with company. The cheapness of the conveyance made it equally commodious for Dead fish and Lively company.

Charles Lamb to Mrs Dyer

(*his last letter*)

DEAR MRS DYER,—I am very uneasy about a *Book* which I either have lost or left at your house on Thursday. It was the book I went out to fetch from Miss Buffam's, while the tripe was frying. It is called *Phillip's Theatrum Poetarum* ; but it is an English book. I think I left it in the parlour. It is Mr Cary's book, and I would not lose it for the world. Pray, if you find it, book it at the Swan, Snow Hill, by an Edmonton stage immediately, directed to Mr Lamb, Church Street, Edmonton, or write to say you cannot find it. I am quite anxious about it. If it is lost, I shall never like tripe again.

With kindest love to Mr Dyer and all.

Postscript

IF every business man were compelled to read over, at the beginning of each day, copies of the letters he dictated one year before, he would see for himself that many of them were twice as long as necessary, and that many were not necessary at all.

CARL CROW

Petrol is a Problem

SINCE petrol rationing came in, many people have found it impossible to use their cars for travelling to and from their offices, as they used to do in the good old days.

This problem concerns four people working in the same office, who overcame the petrol problem by clubbing together and using one car a day between them.

Two of them—A and B—lived twenty miles from the office, and the other two—C and D—only ten miles out.

For the first fortnight, they used the cars belonging to A and B, who drove on alternate days, calling for C and D *en route*. It was agreed that the cost of travelling should be worked out on a mileage basis and that each person should pay his fair share.

At the end of the fortnight, it appeared that A and B had spent on petrol, oil, and other expenses a total of £6 between them.

What proportion of this should be borne by A and B, and what by C and D ?

" *And last night it was so dark I nearly posted my letter in a Chelsea Pensioner !* "

Spare the Rod

AN Arab took his boy to a *mwallimu*, or teacher. " I will pay you well to teach my boy the Koran from the Surah Al Fatihat to the 114th," he said. " The lad is bright, but if he stumbles, do not beat him. Beat instead this little black slave whom I leave with you."

While he had some one to beat, the *mwallimu* did not care. He did as told, with the result that at the end of the term the little black slave knew the Koran by heart, whereas the Arab boy had not even made a dent in the first Surah.

MARIUS FORTIE
in *Black and Beautiful*

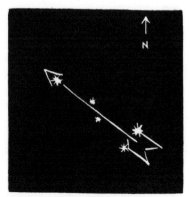

You can't black-out the Stars !

No. 43. *Sagitta* (the Arrow)

A small Northern constellation lying just above Aquila. Otherwise known as Alahance.

Odd Jobs

No. 10. *The Ladybird King*

An American named Peach spends the period between April and July each year capturing tens of thousands of coleopterous beetles—lady-birds to you. These are shipped in specially prepared containers to fruit-growers and rose-growers all over America, who use them for killing the pests which attack rose and fruit trees.

A—Zoo

No. 43. *The Fox*

The Fox
Always wears sox
With clox.

The Shepherd Boy sings in the Valley of Humiliation

HE that is down needs fear no fall,
　He that is low, no pride ;
He that is humble ever shall
　Have God to be his guide.

I am content with what I have,
　Little be it, or much :
And, Lord, contentment still I crave,
　Because Thou savest such.

Fullness to such a burden is
　That go on pilgrimage :
Here little, and hereafter bliss,
　Is best from age to age.
　　　　　　　　JOHN BUNYAN

You can't black-out the Stars!

No. 44. Triangulum
　　(the Triangle)

This is a small constellation lying between Andromeda and Aries.

The Lighter Side of the Black-out

Many persons call a doctor when all they want is an audience.
　　　　　　　　JAMES K. SMITH

★

One thing about a woman's purse—she can always find anything she doesn't want in it !
　　　　　　　　HENRY NEWSON

★

You can say this for Europe—she sticks to her guns !
" CHRISTIAN SCIENCE MONITOR."

★

All matches in Japan have been shortened .029 inches, thus saving £60,000 a year in timber.
　　　　　　　　JOHN GUNTHER

★

A husband is what's left of a sweetheart after the nerve has been killed.
　　　　　　　　VIC OLIVER

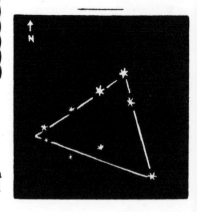

TWO BY TWO

HERE is a more difficult association test still.

Each of the words in List One should be associated in your mind with one of the words in List Two. Can you pair them all off in less than two minutes?

List One

1. Bat.
2. Weeds.
3. Weed.
4. Toast.
5. Titania.
6. Atkins.
7. Paint.
8. Ring.
9. Writ.
10. Ripe.
11. Oil.
12. Emerald.

List Two

A. Army.
B. Book.
C. Tobacco.
D. Cherry.
E. Belfry.
F. Water.
G. Ireland.
H. Dream.
I. Powder.
J. Holy.
K. Widow.
L. Glass.

Truth, and freedom to seek it, are not luxury-products which enervate a people and unfit them for the struggle of life. They belong to life : they are life's daily bread.

THOMAS MANN

A—Zoo

No. 44. The Leopard

Can the Leopard change his spots ? Yes, when he moves from place to place.

OLD RIDDLE

This was Etiquette as

In an old diary of my great-grandmother's, copied out in copperplate, I found these rules governing etiquette. How many of them still

Good manners are made up of petty sacrifices.

*

Do not introduce people in a public conveyance. It draws attention to a person and makes him unpleasantly conspicuous.

*

When calling, do not enter into grave discussions. Trifling subjects are better.

*

It is rude to turn a chair so that your back will be presented to anyone.

*

In company do not converse with another in a language that is not understood by the rest.

*

If it becomes necessary to break a marriage engagement, it is best to do so by letter. The reasons for your course can be given much more clearly than in a personal interview. All presents, letters, etc., received should accompany the letter announcing the termination of the engagement.

*

During a walk in the country, when ascending a hill or walking on the bank of a stream, and the lady is fatigued, and sits upon the ground, a gentleman will not seat himself by her, but remain standing until she is rested sufficiently to proceed.

*

A dispute about religion is foolish. When it is known that there are fifteen hundred millions of people on the face of the earth, speaking 3034 tongues, and possessing one thousand different religious beliefs, it will be easily seen that it is a hopeless task to harmonize them all.

*

Do not eat all on your plate and do not clean it up with your bread.

*

A lady at a ball should not burden a gentleman with her gloves, fan, and bouquet while she dances unless he is her husband or brother.

*

Do not place your arm on the back of a chair occupied by a lady.

*

Ladies can make each other's acquaintance in the hotel parlour, or at the table. It is optional with them how far it is carried.

*

It is not polite at a wedding to

Etiquette was Ticket

The word ' Etiquette ' comes from the same source as ' Ticket.' In fact, in the good old days, it was the ticket of admission to a function ; for these tickets always bore the rules governing behaviour written or printed on the card. Etiquette is nothing more than the French for ticket.

Great Grandmama knew it

apply I leave readers of the " Black-out Book " to decide for themselves. I often wonder how many of them great-grandmama really kept !

congratulate the bride. She should receive wishes for her future happiness. The bridegroom is the one who is to be congratulated. He is the fortunate one.

★

Blowing soup or pouring tea and coffee into the saucer to cool it, is evidence of a lack of knowledge of the usages of good society.

★

When friends call on you, never look to your watch. It appears as if you were desirous that they should go.

★

Never pick the teeth, scratch the head, blow the nose, or clean your nails in company.

★

Never correct the pronunciation of a person publicly ; nor any inaccuracy that may be made in a statement.

★

Do not ask the age of another, unless they are quite youthful. Some very sensible men and women are sensitive on this point. Whether it be considered silly or not, they have a right to keep their secret.

Manners maketh Man

The gentle minde by gentle deeds is knowne ;
For a man by nothing is so well betrayed
As by manners.
EDMUND SPENSER
Manners must adorn knowledge, and smooth its way through the world.
EARL OF CHESTERFIELD

Do not permit a gentleman to remove a bracelet from your arm, or a ring from your finger, for the purpose of examination. Take them off and hand them to him.

★

A lady will not strike a gentleman with her handkerchief, or tap him with her fan.

★

To introduce a person who is in anyway objectionable to a friend, is insulting.

★

Giggling, whispering, staring about in church is a mark of ill-breeding.

★

Do not draw near the fire, when calling, unless invited.

★

A business address should never be seen on a visiting card. A card with a photograph on it is a piece of vulgar conceit.

★

The only gifts which should pass between ladies and gentlemen who are not relatives are books, flowers, music, and confectionery.

★

To pencil your sentiments in a borrowed book is rude.

Take the Consequences!

EVERY-BODY knows the ordinary form of Consequences, and there is no need to describe it here, but there are several other versions of the game which are well worth playing.

These, for example.

They are all played by writing down the first step, folding the paper, and passing it on to the next player, who writes the second, and so on.

1. Last Will and Testament

Each player writes at the top of his paper : " This is the last will and testament of me ——" followed by the name and address of anyone—real or imagined. The papers are then folded and passed on. The second stage is the principal bequest, the third and fourth are subsidiary bequests, the fifth a ' pious sentiment ' or ' dying wish,' the sixth and seventh deal with the appointment of executors, and the eighth is a codicil assumed to be added two years later.

Some very remarkable wills have been written in this game.

2. Bookworm

For those who read a great deal, this is particularly popular. The stages are as follows :

(1) Title of book.
(2) Name of author.
(3) Name of publisher.
(4) Five-line description of contents.
(5) Extract from review by *Times* or *Observer*.
(6) Extract from review by *Daily Mirror* or *Peg's Paper*.
(7) Your own opinion of the book.

3. Sporting Life

This is a safe bet for any type of party, and particularly when there is a larger percentage of men than usual. It consists of a newspaper report of any sporting event, and the principal stages are these :

(1) Headlines.
(2) Introduction. (This must give the main details of the event witnessed by the supposed reporter, including a mention of the particular sport chosen.)
(3) The names of the teams, runners, or opponents.
(4) Five-line description of the play.
(5) The result.
(6) Summing-up by the reporter.

The Swallow

FOOLISH prater, what dost thou
So early at my window do ?
Cruel bird, thou'st ta'en away
A dream out of my arms to-day ;
A dream that ne'er must equall'd be
By all that waking eyes may see.
Thou this damage to repair
Nothing half so sweet and fair,
Nothing half so good, canst bring,
Tho' men say thou bring'st the spring.

ABRAHAM COWLEY

You can't black-out the Stars !

No. 45. Perseus

Named after the classic hero, Perseus, this is one of the oldest northern constellations. It contains Algol, sometimes called the Demon.

Chestnut Corner

No. 10. Photographic

You've probably heard about the enterprising photographer who put up a large notice outside his shop, reading :

DARK ROOM FOR
PHOTOGRAPHY
LOVERS

Developments promised in Two Hours.

One morning he arrived to find a large crowd of young people in front of his shop. The local wag had painted out the word " Photography."

A—Zoo

No. 45. The Goat

*The odour of a Goat
Is never remote.*

WORD PYRAMIDS

HERE'S an amusing way of spending a black-out evening—building up word pyramids.

Just to show you how it's done, here is a very easy one for you to solve :

```
        x
      x   x
    x   x   x
  x   x   x   x
x   x   x   x   x
```

Starting from the top of the pyramid, you have first of all a single letter of the alphabet. Add one letter to it and you have a preposition. Add another and you have what you did at the dining-table to-night. Add one more and your meal is delayed. Add another and you get an object connected with the dining-table we have already mentioned.

Now, can you build up a pyramid like that for yourself? There's no limit to the number of rows—provided that you add only one letter to the existing word each time.

If you wish to, you can re-arrange the existing letters as much as you please.

Odd Jobs

No. 11. Soap Taster and Toe Polisher

At least one man has earned his living for forty years by tasting soap. His name is John Hanser, and his job is to determine the fat and alkali content of the soap.

Another, on the beach at Waikiki, earns his living as an unusual sort of shoeblack. He paints and polishes the toenails of the women bathers.

A—Zoo

No. 46. The Horse

I know two things about the Horse,
And one of them is rather coarse.

ANON.

Strictly Personal
No. 31. Dr Goebbels

Pray consider the case of this poor Dr Goebbels:
In the cause of his Fuehrer he rants and he
* burbles.*
Now his brain from invention's so terribly sore
That he dare not believe his own thoughts any
* more.*

Chestnut Corner

No. 11. Party

The hotel dining-room presented a most unusual appearance. All of the small tables had been evacuated and two very large ones substituted.

" Why the changes ? " I asked.

" There's a party on this evening," said the manager. " Mrs Blessington's invited eighty people to dine here."

" Mrs Blessington ! " I repeated. " Are you sure ? "

" Of course I'm sure," snapped the manager. " Her man rang up and ordered a special table for a party of eighty. He even ordered the menu."

Just then Mrs Blessington was announced, and in a moment she walked slowly in. She certainly must have been at least eighty.

WAITING

THERE has fallen a splendid tear
　　From the passion-flower at the gate.
She is coming, my dove, my dear ;
　　She is coming, my life, my fate ;
The red rose cries, " She is near, she is near " ;
　　And the white rose weeps, " She is late " ;
The larkspur listens, " I hear, I hear " ;
　　And the lily whispers, " I wait."

She is coming, my own, my sweet ;
　　Were it ever so airy a tread,
My heart would hear her and beat,
　　Were it earth in an earthy bed ;
My dust would hear her and beat
　　Had I lain for a century dead ;
Would start and tremble under her feet,
　　And blossom in purple and red.

TENNYSON—*Maud*

ARE YOU REALLY LAZY?

S OME of us are lazy and love it. Some of us are lazy and hotly deny the fact. Some of us (I suppose) are never lazy—although I must say I have never met anyone in the third category.

Here's a little test you can apply to yourself. It will help you to discover whether you are bone lazy, very lazy, or just lazy. Answer the questions as though you were on oath and then consult the score-card below.

1. Do you always answer letters the day you receive them?

2. Do you sometimes leave them so long that eventually they don't need an answer?

3. Have you a carrier for your gas-mask, or do you just carry it around in its box? If you just carry it around in the box, have you fitted a strap or string to it, so that it will hang over your shoulder?

4. Do you always get up directly you are called? Five minutes after? More than ten minutes after?

5. Do you fill your fountain-pen regularly, or wait till the ink has run out? If it runs out, do you then finish the letter you're writing in pencil?

6a. (Men only.) Do you always have your hair cut directly it needs it?

6b. (Girls only.) Do you al-ways sew on a shoulder-strap *directly* it breaks, or do you sometimes use a safety-pin?

7. When you are alone in the house, do you lay a meal for yourself properly, or eat picnic fashion?

8. Do you take a penny bus for short distances you could easily walk when you are not in a hurry?

Now compare your answers with this score-key and see what your score is.

1. 'Yes' adds 10 to your score.

2. 'Yes' subtracts 5 from your score.

3. If you have a carrier, add 10; if you carry it around in a box, subtract 5, but if you have fitted a strap to the box so that it hangs over your shoulder, add 5.

4. At once, add 10; five minutes after, no score; ten minutes or more, subtract 5.

5. 'Yes' to the first question adds 10 to your score. 'Yes' to the second subtracts 5.

6a. 'Yes' adds 5.

6b. 'Yes' adds 5.

7. A properly laid meal wins you 10 more points.

8. If you do, subtract 20.

Now, if you've added up (or subtracted!) your totals, you can compare them with this:

A score of 25 or more means that you have nothing to re-proach yourself with. A score between zero and 20 inclusive means that you are just plain, average lazy, while a score below zero leaves no doubt whatever about it.

Oh, and I forgot to mention that a score of 50 or more means that you're too good to be true!

You can't black-out the Stars !

No. 46. Hercules

Hanging between Lyra and Corona Borealis, this contains a famous cluster in which are more than 5000 suns.

Scots survivor : "*Joost a meenit ! Is there ony charge ?*"

13

Poor Old Horse

OH, once I lay in stable, a
   hunter well and warm,
I had the best of shelter from
   cold and rain and harm ;
But now in open meadow, a
   hedge I'm glad to find,
To shield my sides from tempest, from driving sleet
   and wind.
   Poor old horse, let him die !

My shoulders once were
   sturdy, were glossy,
   smooth and round,
But now, alas ! they're
   rotten, I'm not ac-
   counted sound.
As I have grown so agèd,
   my teeth gone to decay,
My master frowns upon me ;
   I often hear him say,
" Poor old horse, let him
   die ! "

Ye gentlemen of England,
   ye sportsmen good and
   bold,
All ye that love a hunter,
   remember him when
   old ;
Oh, put him in your stable,
   and make the old boy
   warm,
And visit him, and pat him,
   and keep him out of
   harm,
   Poor old horse, till he die.

Old English Song

Let's have Fun and

On these two pages you will find the nucleus of the middle of the left-hand page

Backward Spelling

THIS sounds easy, but it is astonishingly difficult.

All the players have to do is spell a familiar word backward (*i.e.*, if the word is *garden*, they must spell it *nedrag*).

The game is best played with everyone spelling his words aloud in turn. To make the competition quite fair, have a series of easy questions ready. You can ask the players to spell their own names, those of houses or streets in the locality, motor-cars, and so on— all backward.

Progressive Games

WHEN you have a party, or when the whole family happens to be at home at once, try organizing a progressive-games evening. All you need is a programme of eight or nine games—those on this page will give you a start, and there are plenty more elsewhere in the book. Allot 10 or 15 minutes to each and give everybody a score-card. Then those who do not shine at one game have a chance of making up with another and winning the prize—if you decide to offer one.

Shove-ha'penny Bowls

Shove-ha'penny is really a game for two people only, but you can make it four or five a side by playing shove-ha'penny bowls. Stick a pin in the far end of the board and call this the jack. Now the game, as in bowls, is to get your woods (in this case the ha'pence) as near the jack as possible, while knocking your opponents' woods out of the way.

If you don't possess a shove-ha'penny board, play this on a table, with a sixpence for the jack and pennies for the woods.

The game can be played by two teams of four or five (winners sharing the points between them) or you can organize a quick knock-out competition.

Sharing the Petrol

Now for something quieter— a simple little problem. You can give five or ten marks to the one who first solves it correctly and consolation prizes to those who get the right answer later, but within a prescribed time-limit.

It's about two more of those poor, petrol-starved motorists, who were both stranded beside the road without a drop in either's tank. A passing army lorry very considerately gave them an eight-gallon can full of petrol (this has never happened to me, by the way) and drove on.

Games this Evening!

an evening of progressive games. The panel in *tells you how to organize it.*

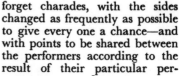

The motorists now wished to divide the petrol equally between them, but found that they had only a three-gallon tin and a five-gallon tin with which to measure it.

Could they do it? And if so, how?

Card Quoits

If you've got anyone who wants to show you card tricks, stop him and show him Card Quoits.

This is played by giving each player an equal number of cards —which should

be of different packs or different suits to differentiate them from one another—and placing a man's hat or a waste-paper basket three or four yards away from the players.

The game is to 'skate' your cards into the hat, and you score according to the number of your cards which go home.

Charades

And we must certainly not forget charades, with the sides changed as frequently as possible to give every one a chance—and with points to be shared between the performers according to the result of their particular performance.

Two useful pointers for charade teams are :

Don't spend too much time dressing up. Simple 'props' like those illustrated here are better than elaborate toilettes. They give an adequate impression—and they give you more time to spend on thinking out your word.

And don't forget to slip in a couple of red herrings—obvious one-letter words which look as though they're going to be the syllables of your final word, but aren't !

Here are three useful words for charade purposes :

CONSTANTINOPLE,
PERQUISITE,
SUPPLEMENT.

Happy party, every one !

ARE YOU QUITE SURE ?

I F you're not, you'll find the correct answers at the back of the book. To make it easier for you, four or five alternative answers are given for every question. All you've got to do is to select the correct one.

1. The two most nutritive root vegetables are —— and the ——.

Beet, carrot, turnip, swede, potato.

2. *Tales from the Vienna Woods* was written by—

Schubert,   Offenbach,   Strauss, Chopin.

3. *Gulliver's Travels* was written by—

Charles Lamb, Jonathan Swift, Daniel Defoe, Lemuel Gulliver.

4. The number of pence piled flat one on top of another necessary to make up the height of a penny standing on its side is—

6, 11, 14, 19, 24.

5. A swan lives on an average about —— years.

10, 16, 24, 50.

6. The area of the world inhabited by human beings is —— square miles.

5 million, 17 million, 50 million, 67 million.

7. The number of tins of foodstuffs sold in Great Britain each year is —— millions.

20, 79, 148, 1600, 5400.

8. Jellyfish are —— per cent. water.

15, 30, 45, 60, 90.

9. There is one old Etonian in Parliament to every —— from other schools.

2, 3, 5, 11, 19.

10. Helium is a—

Precious metal, lighter-than-air gas, Greek city, period of unconsciousness.

A—Zoo

No. 47. The Lobster

*Even a gangster or a mobster
Can be put on the spot by Lobster.*

The Englishman's Wife

During a brush with the Zulus in the last Zulu war, the Scots were in action and fought particularly well. After the battle a captured Zulu was heard to remark : " Wow ! The Englishman, he can fight—but his wife ! Wow ! "

You can't black-out the Stars !

No. 47. Camelopardalus

(the Giraffe)

A small northern constellation

situated between Cepheus, Ursa Major, and Draco.

THE DEVIL'S WALK

ONCE, early in the morning,
  Beelzebub arose,
With care his sweet person adorning,
  He put on his Sunday clothes.

He drew on a boot to hide his hoof,
  He drew on a glove to hide his claw,
His horns were concealed by a *Bras Chapeau*,
And the Devil went forth as natty a *Beau*
  As Bond Street ever saw.

He sate him down, in London town,
  Before earth's morning ray ;
With a favourite imp he began to chat,
On religion, and scandal, this and that,
  Until the dawn of day.

P. B. SHELLEY

Don't play Cards with Strangers!

THE one piece of advice every wise father gives his son is, "Don't play cards with strangers!"

In case any son thinks he is wiser than his wise father, he should read this authoritative account of what happened when Michael MacDougall, the 'card detective,' played bridge with two recognized experts.

The match—a special demonstration affair—took place at the Cavendish Club, New York, in November, 1938.

Before MacDougall played a game with Howard Schenkin and B. Jay Becker as opponents, two ordinary packs were thoroughly mixed and handed to the players. MacDougall shuffled the blue pack and Schenken the red. After the red pack had been well mixed it was cut by Becker, and dealt

by MacDougall. Before dealing, MacDougall announced that he would bid six no-trumps. With 100 pairs of eyes fastened on his hands, he dealt and made six no-trumps.

Then Schenken dealt the blue pack. This had been in full view from the time it was given to MacDougall to shuffle. Nevertheless, after the cards had been cut and dealt, MacDougall received all 13 spades.

MacDougall accomplished it all by expert manipulation of the cards during the pick-up of played hands, the shuffle, and the deal.

Now let's all have a nice friendly game of Rummy, shall we?

The Key of the Kingdom

HERE is the Key of the Kingdom!
In that kingdom there is a town ;
In that town there is a street ;
In that street there is a lane ;
In that lane there is a court ;
In that court there is a house ;
In that house there is a room ;
In that room there is a bed ;
On that bed there lies a child :
And that child has the Key of the Kingdom.

ANON

A—Zoo
No. 48. The Hyena

Few Esquimaux have seen a Hyena.

How to cash Cheques

This is a very old trick, but it always finds fresh admirers. Tell a friend that with only ten bundles of pound notes you could cash him a cheque for any sum he cared to mention in pounds, from £1 to £1000, without breaking into any of the bundles.

He will not believe you, but it can be done. All you need is to have £1 in the first bundle, £2 in the second, and so on, doubling the amount each time until you reach £512.

Try it with ten slips of paper marked with the amounts and you will find that you can make up any figure you like from one to one thousand, simply by putting so many of the bundles together.

You can't black-out the Stars !

No. 48. Canis Minor
(the Little Dog)

This constellation follows Orion to the south of Gemini. Named after the faithful dog of Icarus, it contains one fine star, Procyon.

DARKNESS AND LIGHT

DARKNESS brings weariness, question, mystery and silence ; with light comes bustling life, understanding, and fresh courage. I watched Morning at her housework ; she brushed back the darkness into the countless cellars of the marshes and deeps of the waters ; she snatched the blankets of mist from the lie-a-beds ; she opened the shutters and flung wide the door ; the universe shone with her energy. Her bustle roused the world's myriad citizens ; there was a flutter of wings and a twinkling of eyes, of a sudden the world was agog with life. There was singing in the wood, laughter in the water, movement on the hills, a yawning in the valley—the world was awake. . . .

NANCY PRICE—*The Gull's Way*

Are You Truthful!

DO you think you are a truthful person?

You do?

Then answer the following list of questions—but answer them truthfully, of course!

You may prefer to do this in private and tot up your marks before you answer the questions publicly.

Here they are:

1. Have you ever said: "I really haven't a thing to wear!"?

2. Can you think of a single occasion on which you have said: "Of course, I remember you quite well——" when all the time you just couldn't place the person in question?

3. Do you always mean exactly what you say, when you thank a person for a gift, like this: "Thank you so much—it's exactly what I wanted"?

4. Have you ever told an inquirer personally, or over the telephone: "Sorry, Mr So-and-So is out"?

5. Do you always mean it when you murmur: "I've enjoyed myself so much. It was sweet of you to ask us. It's been a lovely evening"?

6. Or when you add: "And you must come and spend an evening with us very soon. We're so looking forward to having you!"?

If you answer "Yes" to 1, 2, 4, or "No" to 3, 5, 6, then you obviously cannot be one hundred per cent. truthful. But don't worry too much—you'll still be in the majority!

The Truth about Women

When I have one foot in the grave I will tell the truth about women. I shall tell it, jump into my coffin, pull the lid over me, and say, "Do what you like now." TOLSTOY

A—Zoo
No. 49. The Lizard

*The thought of a Lizard
Sticks in my gizzard.*

A Robin Redbreast in a Cage

A ROBIN redbreast in a cage
 Puts all heaven in a rage ;
A dog starved at his master's gate
Predicts the ruin of the State ;
A game-cock clipped and armed
  for fight
Doth the rising sun affright ;
A horse misused upon the road
Calls to heaven for human blood ;
Each outcry of the hunted hare
A fibre from the brain doth tear ;
A skylark wounded on the wing
Doth make a cherub cease to sing ;
He who shall hurt the little wren
Shall never be beloved by men ;
The beggar's dog and widow's
  cat,
Feed them and thou shalt grow
  fat.

WILLIAM BLAKE

Strictly Personal

No. 32. Hore Belisha

The patron saint of English roads
 He will be praised in song and story.
Yet all his beacons and his codes
 Don't stop the roads from being gory.

Rod, Pole, and Perch

Do you know all about so many so-and-so making one rod, pole, or perch ?

If you do, here is a very simple little sum for you.

From 10 poles 1 yard 1 foot subtract 9 poles 6 yards 2 feet 6 inches.

It's a simple sum when you know how.

You can't black-out the Stars !

No. 49. Canis Major
(the Great Dog)

A constellation which follows Orion. It contains the great white star called Sirius, or the ' Dog Star.'

Here comes the Bride!

The reason why so few marriages are happy is because young ladies spend their time in making nets, not in making cages.
SWIFT

The Bride wept

For many years in this country it was ' the thing ' for a bride to weep at her wedding. Now, of course, that privilege is reserved for the bride's mother.

The bride's tears were due to a notion that the marriage would be unhappy if she did not weep at the wedding—and this in turn was due to the belief that a witch could not shed more than three tears, and all of those from her left eye. If the bride wept copiously, it assured her husband that she was no witch.

★

Wedding Anniversary

The wedding anniversaries all have their own particular names. The principal ones are :

5th anniversary . *Wooden Wedding.*
10th anniversary . *Tin wedding.*
15th anniversary . *Crystal wedding.*
20th anniversary . *China wedding.*
25th anniversary . *Silver wedding.*
50th anniversary . *Golden wedding.*
60th anniversary . *Diamond wedding.*

So if you know some one who has been married exactly five years, send her something made out of wood !

Fidelity

If two normal people love each other and marry young, it is likely that for the first seven years fidelity will be easy for both. In the second seven years the time of trial may come for either, but it is more likely to come to the man, and will be more severe in his case. (It may be observed in parentheses that it is as wise to demand the same morality in both sexes as to demand the same physique, but not wiser.) Fidelity that has survived for fifteen years will probably survive for life.

BARRY PAIN

★

Triumph

The bridal wreath at a wedding is a direct descendant of the crown of triumph worn by the ancient Greeks.

★

Ventilation

Marriage should be ventilated every so often by separation ; but not so much ventilation that it becomes a draught.

ROSITA FORBES

Wedding Wit and Wisdom

A young man married is a young man marred.
SHAKESPEARE

Married in haste, we may repent at leisure.
CONGREVE

Expensive Wedding Present

A young married couple who had just settled down in their new home got a pleasant surprise in their mail one morning—a couple of tickets for one of the best shows in town. But the donor had omitted to send his name. With the tickets was a slip of paper, bearing the words : " Guess who from ? "

They enjoyed the show ; but when they reached home, they found that all their wedding presents had been taken. There was a note from the burglar, saying : " Now you know."

★

Suggested Addition to the Marriage Service

" I do solemnly promise thee that if I am tempted to run away with another person I will first run away with thee for at least two weeks and to some place where we can again be as intimately and exclusively each other's as we will be on our coming honeymoon, so help me God ! "

★

The Ring

Do you know why a ring is given in marriage ? Because originally the ring bore a seal, and the bridegroom, by handing the ring to his wife, vested in her the right to use his seal. The third finger of the left hand was chosen because the Romans believed that a nerve ran from that finger direct to the heart.

★

Crazy Wedding

Charles Durande, a wealthy Louisiana plantation owner, determined to give his two daughters the most spectacular wedding in history. From China he ordered a shipload of spiders, which were released in the mile-long avenue of great pine trees leading up to the house. As the day for the double wedding drew near, the trees were webbed with thousands of yards of filmy lace. Couriers brought from California hundreds of pounds of silver and gold dust ; and Negro slaves with hand-operated bellows sprayed the glittering metal over the webs.

More than two thousand guests marched beneath this glittering fairy canopy to an altar erected in front of the mansion.

ANDRÉ OLIVIER

THE
SENSE
OF SMELL

IT is always strange to me when people regard their sense of smell as of so little worth. There is nothing that can so vividly induce memory; it not only recalls the past but gives it life. It is one of my chief physical pleasures, and without it three-quarters of the joy of a garden would go. The scent of a red rose, a tea rose, a wild rose, sweetbriar, mignonette, a lavender bush, a honeysuckle hedge, a bank of sweet violets, a bed of lilies of the valley, cowslips, new-mown hay, cut grass, the mimosa tree; the fragrance of may and lilac, the whole countryside in spring, the earth after rain, wild thyme on a Sussex Down, and not only the fragrant smells but the invigorating scent of sea, pine, heather, peat, the comfortable smell of burning wood, and the appetizing smells of roasting coffee, baking bread, and savoury dishes—to smell none of these things would to me rob life of much enjoyment.

NANCY PRICE—*The Gull's Way*

★   ★   ★

" *James Mitchell was deaf, dumb and blind from birth, but he distinguished persons by their smell, and by means of the same sense formed correct judgments as to their character.*"

NINETEENTH CENTURY

Two-minute Test

IN less than two minutes, you ought to be able to rearrange the items given below, so that each is opposite its usual complement. Of course there are possible doubts—*fish* might be paired off with either 7 or 9, but you'll soon find that it must be 7.

A	knife	— salt	1
B	sausage	— cup	2
C	fish	— coat	3
D	pepper	— socks	4
E	hat	— mash	5
F	brace	— butter	6
G	elephant	— chips	7
H	bread	— bit	8
I	egg	— fork	9
J	shoes	— castle	10

Strictly Personal

No. 33. Anthony Eden

The voice that breathes o'er Eden's sure to be
Attended to with suave civility,
But underneath the hat the head's a hard 'un—
You cannot lead this Eden up the garden.

You can't black-out the Stars !

No. 50. Canes Venatici
(the Hunting Dogs)

A small northern constellation between Bootes and Ursa Major.

Chestnut Corner

No. 12. Shaw, Sir !

An admiral is said once to have asked George Bernard Shaw :

" Can you tell me who, in your opinion, is the most eminent playwright of the century ? "

To which Shaw, without hesitation, replied :

" Ay, ay, sir ! "

MIXED BAG

ERE'S a handful of easy little puzzles and problems from the back pages of my notebook. Among them there must be at least one you haven't heard before :

1. When you say that a man wrought ' something or other, what is the verb you are using ? Or, to put it another way, of what verb is ' wrought ' the past participle ?

2. A schoolboy once wrote that a man had become ' bankrupt and insolent.' What did he really mean ?

3. How many rhymes would you say there are for ' nose ' ? (Dictionary words only, of course.)

4. And how many for ' altar ' ?

5. There are approximately 360,000 marriages a year. Assuming that there are 6000 divorces, would it be correct to say that there are 708,000 more married people at the end of the year than at the beginning ?

6. What is a missal ?

7. Who were the Borgias, and for what were they noted ?

8. This one is for the children. Here are three simple words :

DAD   GOT   CAN

Can you rearrange them to make three other words, including the names of two animals often grouped together ?

9. Here's a harder one for the older members of the family. These three words contain two fish. Can you find them ?

IRE   CAP   CLAP

10. Two motorists were talking, and one asked the other how much petrol he was allowed. The other replied, jokingly : " Well, if I had as much again and half as much again and fifteen gallons, I should have the same number as the horse-power of your car." If the first motorist had a 30 h.p. car, how much petrol was the other allowed ?

" *Wonder who's been billeted in the haunted room ?* "

A—Zoo

No. 50. The Armadillo

*The Armadillo
Prefers a hard pillow.*

Odd Jobs

No. 12. Spider-farmer

You don't like spiders? M. Grantavie does. They happen to be his livelihood. He keeps about ten thousand on his spider farm, all of the type which spin those marvellous large webs. What does he do with them? Sells them at about sixpence each, in lots of one hundred, to wine merchants who want their bottles to look thoroughly old!

THE GRASSHOPPER

O THOU that swing'st upon the waving hair
　　Of some well-filled oaten beard,
Drunk every night with a delicious tear
　　Dropt thee from heaven, where thou wert reared!

The joys of earth and air are thine entire,
　　That with thy feet and wings dost hop and fly;
And when thy poppy works, thou dost retire
　　To thy carved acorn-bed to lie.

Up with the day, the sun thou welcom'st then,
　　Sport'st in the gilt plaits of his beams,
And all these merry days mak'st merry men,
　　Thyself, and melancholy streams.

RICHARD LOVELACE

Famous Last Words

Lord Nelson

" Kismet, Hardy." (*No, Bobby, he didn't say " Kiss me, Hardy." That is just one of those superstitions that sometimes find their way into history books.*)

*

Julius Cæsar

" Et tu, Brute ? " (*According to Shakespeare.*)

*

Beethoven

" I shall hear in heaven ! "

*

Nero

" What an artist the world is losing in me ! "

Cleopatra

" As sweet as balm, as soft as air, as gentle—
O Antony ! "
(*According to Shakespeare.*)

*

Anne Boleyn

" The executioner, they say, is very expert, and my neck is very slender."

*

Palmerston

" Die, my dear doctor ? That is the *last* thing I shall do ! "

*

Any Motorist

" I bet I can get her to do ninety."

SUMMER IS COMING

" SUMMER is coming, summer is coming.
    I know it, I know it, I know it.
Light again, leaf again, life again, love again,"
    Yes, my wild little Poet.
Sing the new year in under the blue.
    Last year you sang it as gladly.
" New, new, new, new ! " Is it then *so* new
    That you should carol so madly?
" Love again, song again, nest again, young again,"
    Never a prophet so crazy !
And hardly a daisy as yet, little friend,
    See, there is hardly a daisy.
" Here again, here, here, here, happy year " !
    Oh warble unchidden, unbidden !
Summer is coming, is coming, my dear,
    And all the winters are hidden.

TENNYSON—*The Throstle*

WHERE TO FIND THE STARS

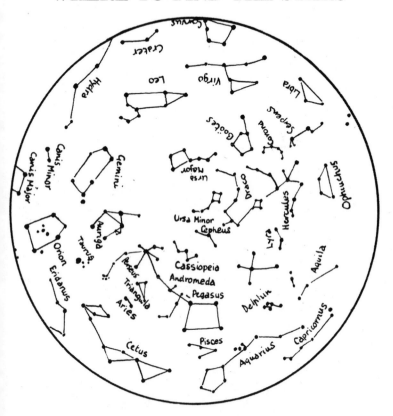

This map of the northern heavens will enable you to find most of the larger constellations given in the " You can't black-out the Stars ! " series. Some of the smaller ones have been omitted, and so, of course, have those which are only visible south of the Equator.

ANSWERS TO PROBLEMS

Page 8 : This is how the men re-arranged themselves so that the sergeant should not notice any difference in their number :

Page 12 : 1. All of them. 2. ½ inch. 3. Medical men give varying figures, ranging from 206 to 270. If you gave either of these you were right. 4. Psaltery, Harmonica, Euphonium, Euphonicon, Bassoon. 5. 4 miles. 6. Kipling ; *Recessional* ; " God of our fathers, known of old." 7. 17 people. 8. $\frac{1}{100}$. 9. 4.

Page 16 : 1. (*a*) Lioness ; (*b*) Tigress ; (*c*) Wolf ; (*d*) Hind ; (*e*) Hen. 2. (*a*) Boar ; (*b*) Ram ; (*c*) Stallion ; (*d*) Gander ; (*e*) Fox.

3. (*a*) Calf ; (*b*) Cub ; (*c*) Gosling ; (*d*) Cygnet ; (*e*) Foal or Colt. 4. (*a*) Shoal ; (*b*) Murmuration ; (*c*) Covey ; (*d*) Gaggle ; (*e*) Flock. 5. (*a*) Byre ; (*b*) Loft or Cote ; (*c*) Lodge ; (*d*) Pen or Fold ; (*e*) Eyrie. 6. (*a*) Crow ; (*b*) Caw ; (*c*) Bray ; (*d*) Hoot ; (*e*) Howl.

Page 19 : 1. Marylebone Cricket Club. 2. Metropolitan Water Board. 3. Member of the Royal College of Surgeons. 4. Milk Marketing Board. 5. London County Council. 6. Member of the Royal College of Physicians. 7. *Black-out Book*. 8. Independent Labour Party. 9. Irish Republican Army. 10. Bachelor of Medicine. 11. Member of Parliament. 12. Prime Minister. 13. Postmaster-General. 14. Automobile Association. 15. Amateur Athletic Association.

The three meanings of ' P.C.' are Privy Councillor, Police Constable, and Post Card.

Page 20 :

$11+1+1+1=14.$ $99+\frac{9}{9}=100.$
$5+\frac{5}{5}+\cdot5=6\frac{1}{2}.$ Six.

Page 24 : This is how the farmer divided the land :

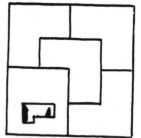

Page 26 : 1. 102. 2. 300,000. 3. Thackeray. 4. 28. 5. 750,000. 6. Nine million. 7. More. 8. 72. 9. Smaller. 10. 2134.

Page 27 : There were 15 fathers in the street.

The father is 28 and the son 10.

Page 29 : There are eight squares in the design, and you reduce the number to four like this :

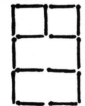

Page 32 : The Air-Raid Wardens were husband and wife. The party in the car consisted of two sisters who had married two brothers and each had a daughter.

Page 33 :

P	R	O	D
L	O	V	E
O	V	E	N
T	E	N	T

Page 35 : The sixteen matches make 10 triangles, but take away 4 like this and there are only 4.

Page 38 : Catapult, Catherine, cathedral, catechism, Catholic, category, caterer, catalogue, catgut.

Page 39 : The complete word diamond and square read :

```
        C
      M O W
    M O L A R
  C O L O N E L
    W A N E D
      R E D
        L
```

```
B  L  A  N  K
A  L  A  R  M
C  L  A  S  H
P  L  A  C  E
S  L  A  C  K
```

The matches make 14 squares and you reduce that to 2 like this :

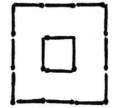

Page 40 : 1. A coot. 2. Ink. 3. A drum. 4. Water. 5. The hills. 6. Gold. 7. A fox. 8. Lead. 9. A berry. 10. Air. 11. A kitten. 12. Pitch. 13. A poker. 14. A peacock. 15. A pikestaff. 16. A bat. 17. Ice. 18. A cucumber. 19. Iron. 20. A glove.

Page 41 : This is how you make five rows of four :

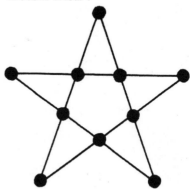

Page 43 : T O B A C C O.

Page 49 : Two by Two—Move 2 and 3 to the farther side of 8 ; move 5 and 6 to take their places ; move 8 and 2 to the places vacated by 5 and 6 ; move the two lumps of sugar from the left and place them in two vacant spaces.

The tradesman was the coal merchant, and what he meant was :

If the grate be empty put coal on.

If the grate be full stop putting coal on.

Page 52 : Telescope, 10s. 4d. ; Book, 3s. 6d. ; Postage, 1s. 4d.

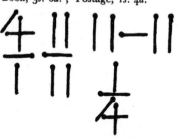

Page 54 : Train A deposits its six coaches in the siding and joins train B, which now consists of two engines and six coaches. This steams past the siding, then backs and picks up the six coaches from there. Our train now consists of two engines, followed by twelve coaches. This is backed past the siding. Engine A is now detached and enters the siding while engine B pulls all twelve coaches past the opening to the siding. Engine A reappears, picks up its own six coaches, and both trains continue their journey.

Page 56 : The handyman blacked out the window like this :

Page 58 : The steps are cut up and the square made like this :

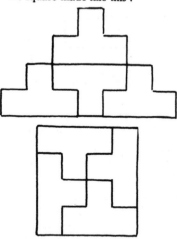

The missing statesmen are :

1. Gamelin.
2. Gort.
3. Chamberlain.
4. Churchill.
5. Hore-Belisha.
6. Eden.
7. Hitler.

Page 62 : The correct quotations are :

1. One touch of nature makes the whole world kin.
2. The quality of mercy is not strain'd ;
   It droppeth as the gentle rain from Heaven.
3. How are the mighty fallen in the midst of the battle !
4. Farewell, a long farewell, to all my greatness !
5. The evil that men do lives after them,
   The good is oft interred with their bones.
6. Sleep, that knits up the ravell'd sleave of care.
7. O sleep ! it is a gentle thing, Beloved from pole to pole.

8. Drink to me only with thine eyes,
   And I will pledge with mine.
9. Not a drum was heard, not a funeral note
   As his corse to the rampart we hurried.
10. Nor hell a fury like a woman scorned.
11. "Why, that I cannot tell," said he ;
    "But 'twas a famous victory."
12. When Britain first, at Heaven's command
    Arose from out the azure main.
The lines which follow "O woman," etc., are :
   And variable as the shade
   By the light quivering aspen made.

Page 64 : The number of triangles in the drawing is 24.

Page 67 : You might accept his offer, but he could never completely pay you back on the terms stated, as you'll find if you work it out—he'd always owe you half of the previous instalment.

Page 68 :

Page 69 : Wherever you start with this problem, there is a possible solution. Here is one variation to prove that it can be done. Assume that the vertical lines of your board are numbered 1–8 and the horizontal lines A–H. Place your pawns or lumps of sugar on the following squares : A5, B2, C4, D6, E8, F3, G1, H7.

Page 70 : 1. Jack-tar ; 2. Jackdaw ; 3. Jacket ; 4. Jackass ; 5. Flapjack ; 6. Jackal ; 7. Jackboot ; 8. Jack-

knife ; 9. Cheapjack ; 10. Jacka-napes.

Page 75 : The sentences when punctuated end at : Mile, home, them, law, conditions, show, success, tzar.

Page 76 :
   1. Shakespeare.
   2. Gladstone.
   3. Duke of Wellington.
   4. Disraeli.
   5. Clemenceau and Gort.
   6. Gladstone.
   7. The Victoria, after Queen Victoria.
   8. Bismarck.
   9. Lincoln.
   10. Cardinal Wolsey.
   11. Châteaubriand.
   12. Prince Albert.

Page 77 :

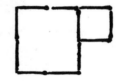

Page 80 : 1. Bench ; 2. Fleet ; 3. School ; 4. Forest ; 5. Clump ; 6. Congregation ; 7. Crew ; 8. Suite ; 9. Board ; 10. Bench ; 11. Catch or Shoal ; 12. Library ; 13. Tribe ; 14. Panel.

Page 82 : The false step is *adding* the lift-boy's 2s. to the 12s. paid by the girls. They paid a total of 12s. (not 15s.), of which the landlord got 10s. and the lift-boy 2s.

Page 86 : 1. No ; 2. No ; 3. Yes ; 4. Yes ; 5. No ; 6. No ; 7. Yes ; 8. Yes ; 9. No ; 10. Yes ; 11. Yes ; 12. Yes ; 13. No ; 14. Yes ; 15. Yes.

Page 87 : Blunderbuss (B.L under 'bus).

Page 89 :

Page 95 : 1. The numbers are 5, 6, 7. 2. 25. 3. 15.

Page 103 : This one is a catch, depending on a very bad pun with the word 'match.' Here's the answer :

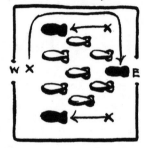

Page 104 : The words should be paired as follows : 1 & H ; 2 & D ; 3 & F ; 4 & J ; 5 & K ; 6 & A ; 7 & C ; 8 & B ; 9 & G ; 10 & E ; 11 & L ; 12 & I.

Page 106 : The balloons were re-arranged like this (you will see that only three were moved) :

Page 108 :

Page 114 : The words should be paired as follows : 1 & E ; 2 & I ; 3 & K ; 4 & H ; 5 & J ; 6 & L ; 7 & A ; 8 & C ; 9 & G ; 10 & F ; 11 & D ; 12 & B.

Page 116 : The new beat Mr Watkins worked out for himself was like this :

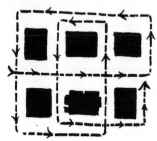

Page 122 : 1. Abode of peace ; 2. A Mohamedan theologian ; 3. 65,000 ; 4. 18 ; 5. 580 ; 6. 5000 ; 7. 60 ; 8. Eucalyptus ; 9. 220 ; 10. A Japanese suicide.

Page 126 : The words should be paired like this : 1 & D ; 2 & K ; 3 & G ; 4 & I ; 5 & E ; 6 & B ; 7 & L ; 8 & H ; 9 & A ; 10 & F ; 11 & C ; 12 & J.

Page 131 : The articles are : Apple, Boy, Candle, Daisy, Elephant, Fireplace, Girl, Hat, Ink, Jumper, Knife, Lemon, Matches, Negro, Orange, Plate, Queen, Rope, Shoe, Table, Umbrella, Vase, Window, Xylophone, Yacht, Zebra.

Page 132 : 1. Darby ; 2. Troilus ; 3. Swan ; 4. Perseus ; 5. Mutt ; 6. Antony or Cæsar ; 7. Jekyll ; 8. Flanagan ; 9. David ; 10. Dante ; 11. Castor ; 12. William or Joseph.

Page 134 :

1. North Atlantic ; South Atlantic ; North Pacific ; South Pacific ; Arctic ; Antarctic ; Indian.

2. The doorkeeper at the House of Commons at the end of a sitting. It was originally the signal to the link-boys and coachmen to prepare to escort the members home.

3. The caret is a printer's sign like this ∧ used to denote that something is missing.

4. He was hanged for treason.

5. Because they have the right to consult the King in his private cabinet at the Palace.

6. Puck.

Page 140 : The solicitor produced a pearl of his own which the old lady had given him during her lifetime and added it to the nineteen, making a total of twenty. He then gave Mary half (10), Marjorie a quarter (5), and May one-fifth (4), making a total of 19, and took his own pearl back again. As he tactfully pointed out to the girls, one-half, one-quarter and one-fifth do not add up to one, which explained why the division had appeared so difficult.

Page 142 : 1. The Harvest Moon (one does not hunt until the harvest is in). 2. ½d. 3. If you rearrange the letters, you'll find that they spell 'Alfred Tennyson, Poet Laureate.' 4. Watchman. 5. Asia, Amazon, Pacific, Simplon. 6. Squirrel fur (Camel was the name of their inventor). 7. Rearrange the two names and you'll find that they make STALIN and FINLAND. The rest of the answer you will find in your newspapers ! 8. Add the letter ' E ' several times, and you will get ' To be perfect, persevere ! ' 9. Rome was not built in a day. 10. Sleeplessness.

Page 148 : 1. Quite easily. The legatees were a grandmother, her daughter, and her grand-daughter. 2. 14⅛ seconds. (In striking four, there are only three pauses, each of them 1⅜ seconds long ; in striking twelve, there will be eleven pauses—or eleven times 1⅜ seconds.) 3. 15½. (If 20 equalled 33, one-fifth of 50, *i.e.,* 10, would be exactly half of that.)

Page 153 :

4	3	8
9	5	1
2	7	6

Page 154 : Seven days. (The tank would be quite full when he poured in the two gallons on the seventh day.)

Page 156 : 1. Katherine ; 2. John ; 3. Wat ; 4. Catherine, The Fair Maid of Perth ; 5. John ; 6. Thomas : 7. John ; 8. Thomas ; 9. Helen ; 10. Anne.

Page 163 : If you look at books on a shelf you will see that the first page of Volume One would be much nearer the last page of Volume Four than you might think. The bookworm actually travelled through six covers and only two volumes, a total of 3½ inches.

Page 166 :

1. BIND	2. BLACK
WIND	SLACK
WAND	STACK
WANE	STALK
LANE	STALE
	SHALE
	WHALE
	WHILE
	WHITE

Page 168 : 1. From its inventor, Henry Shrapnel. 2. A meeting at Lynch's Creek in the eighteenth century, at which an organization known as ' The Regulators ' was formed. 3. The Armenians. 4. 90. 5. No. Germany calculates a circle as 400 degrees and a right-angle, therefore, as 100. 6. 500,000. 7. 7200. 8. The organism by which your tongue tastes food. Your tongue has about 3000—and a cow's tongue about 15,000 ! 9. One-tenth. 10. Three years.

Page 175 : 1. T, A, and I. 2. Z, X, and Q. 3. Five consonants to three vowels. 4. S, C, and P. 5. X, Z, and Y. 6. R, S, T, and D. 7. I, A, and perhaps O if we include poetry. 8. An, at, on, of. 9. And, the.

Page 178 : 1. Sue. 2. Emits. 3. Lilt. 4. Sore. 5. Starer. 6. Capes. There are alternatives to some of these, of course.

Page 182 : A and B should pay 45*s.* each and C and D 15*s.* each.

Page 185 : The words should be paired like this—1 & E ; 2 & K ; 3 & C ; 4 & L ; 5 & H ; 6 & A ; 7 & I ; 8 & B ; 9 & J ; 10 & D ; 11 & F ; 12 & G.

Page 190 :

```
      A
     A T
    A T E
   L A T E
  P L A T E
```

Page 195 : To share the petrol, the motorists used their three receptacles like this (the three columns show how much was in each of the tins at each operation) :

The 8-Gallon	The 5-Gallon	The 3-Gallon
8	–	–
3	5	–
3	2	3
6	2	–
6	–	2
1	5	2
1	4	3
4	4	–

Page 196 : 1. Beet and potato. 2. Strauss. 3. Swift. 4. Nineteen. 5. Fifty. 6. Fifty million. 7. 1600. 8. Ninety. 9. Five. 10. Lighter-than-air gas.

Page 201 : What you have to remember is that 5½ yards make one rod, pole, or perch. Take this into account, and you'll find that the two amounts are exactly equal !

Page 205 : The correct pairings are—D & 1 ; I & 2 ; E & 3 ; J & 4 ; B & 5 ; H & 6 ; C & 7 ; F & 8 ; A & 9 ; G & 10.

Page 206 : 1. To work. 2. Insolvent. 3. 103. 4. Ten. 5. No, because some married people are bound to die during the year. 6. A Roman Catholic mass-book. 7. Fifteenth-century Italian nobles, noted for the number and ingenious method of their murders. 8. Cat and dog. 9. Carp, plaice. 10. Six gallons.